OAKWOOD LIBRARY OF RAILWAY HISTORY

BRICKS AND

THE STRABATHIE LIGHT RAILWAY
AND MURCAR BUGGY

A. Gordon Pirie

A brick manufactured at Strabathie, after being impressed with the manufacturer's name in the frog.
courtesy Ian Suddaby & Mark Cranston

THE OAKWOOD PRESS

ISBN 978-0-85361-765-5

Printed by
Claro Print, Office 26, 27, 1 Spiersbridge Way,
Thornliebank, Glasgow G46 8NG

Thomas Sim, railcar driver, poses in uniform at the Bridge of Don terminus sometime between 1919 and 1922. There is no specific mention of any items of uniform being supplied by the club at this time. Later drivers didn't wear any special clothing so we can surmise he provided them himself. The photograph neatly illustrates the cheek by jowl existence of the brick company and the golf club. A sizeable stack of bricks awaits onward distribution. Just behind the vehicle is one of the brick wagons.
courtesy Norman Sim and family

Published by
The Oakwood Press, 54-58 Mill Square, Catrine, KA5 6RD
Telephone: 01290 551122   Website: www.stenlake.co.uk

Contents

Chapters

Appendices

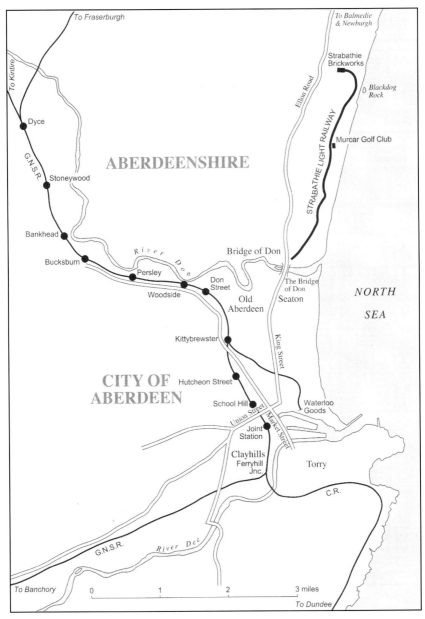

To Fraserburgh

To Kintore

To Balmedie & Newburgh

Strabathie Brickworks

Blackdog Rock

Dyce

Ellon Road

STRABATHIE LIGHT RAILWAY

G.N.S.R.

ABERDEENSHIRE

Stoneywood

Murcar Golf Club

Bankhead

River Don

Bridge of Don

NORTH

Bucksburn

Persley

Don Street

The Bridge of Don

SEA

Woodside

Old Aberdeen

Seaton

Kittybrewster

King Street

CITY OF
ABERDEEN

Hutcheon Street

School Hill

Waterloo Goods

Union Street

Market Street

Joint Station

Clayhills
Ferryhill Jnc.

Torry

C.R.

To Banchory

0   1   2   3 miles

G.N.S.R.

River Dee

To Dundee

Map of the Aberdeen area showing the Strabathie Light Railway in relation to the main line railways: the Great North of Scotland Railway and the Caledonian Railway.

map created by the Author

4

Introduction

This narrow-gauge railway was built in 1899 by the Seaton Brick and Tile Company Limited from the brickworks at Strabathie to Bridge of Don on the northern outskirts of Aberdeen. The Murcar Links Golf Club Limited was granted running powers and operated its own railcar known as the "Murcar Buggy" from their clubhouse to Bridge of Don. When the brickworks closed in 1924 the southern portion of the line was taken over by Murcar Golf Club. Regular services ceased in 1950.

Acknowledgements

I would like to thank staff and members of Aberdeen City Archives, Aberdeen City Council Library and Information Services, University of Aberdeen, National Library of Scotland, Mitchell Library, Birmingham City Council Central Library, Newcastle City Council Libraries, Bodleian Libraries, University of Oxford, Armley Mills Industrial Museum, National Railway Museum, Narrow Gauge Railway Society, The Great North of Scotland Railway Association, Aberdeen Transport Society, Murcar Links Golf Club, Dunecht Estates, and the following individuals who have helped me:

Leslie Darbyshire, John Hill, Russell Wear, Bob Darvill, Allen Civil, Allan Baker, Mike Kennard, Jim Peden, Ronald Redman, Harold S. Bishop (Bud), Mike Mitchell, Ian Souter, David Corstorphine, E.N.C. Haywood, Keith Fenwick, Bob Matthews, Keith Jones, John Daniels, Ronnie MacAskill, Gerald Joss, Norman Sim, Bill Tough, Dick Riddoch, Bob Ballantyne, M. R. Sidney Edwards, Bill McHardy, John S. Reid, Alan W. Brotchie, Keith Turner, Vivienne Forrest, Susan Welsh, Kath Cassidy, Alan Burgess, Bob O'Hara, Neil Parkhouse, Ian Pope, Richard Stenlake, John Alsop, Thelma G. Watt, Connie Leith, Alan Simpson, Jim Livingstone, Jim Fiddes, Jim Rae, Rod Garner, Ian Lord, Bill Brown, Alastair McLeish, Sydney A. Leleux, Wilma Donald, Lawson Little, Ashley Birch, Steve Price, Brian H. Watt, George Mauchline, Ian Suddaby, Mark Cranston

Alexander Christie, Junior manager of the Seaton Brick and Tile Company Limited. He planned the new brickworks at Strabathie and was instrumental in the planning and building of the Strabathie Light Railway.

courtesy
The British Clayworker

Below: A fine new granite head office for the Seaton Brick and Company Limited was opened at 180/182 Market Street in 1898. The option of using brick, even for a brick company was prohibited.

A. Gordon Pirie

Chapter One

The Seaton Brick & Tile Co.

The Seaton Brick & Tile Co. started life in the Seaton area of Aberdeen where the clay-beds had been excavated for centuries. From the 1830s Alexander Nicol, a local businessman, was the chief proprietor of The Seaton Brickworks. The business prospered under brothers Alexander and Charles Christie who were given the positions of joint managers in the 1850s. From 1864 the business was known as The Seaton Brick and Tile Company.

Brickworks also produced pipes, pots and tiles. The production of agricultural drainage tiles was an important aspect of agricultural improvement in Scotland. Drainage tiles had originally consisted of two pieces, the top piece being an inverted "U" or horseshoe-shaped section resting on a separate flat "sole" tile. Later, the introduction of machinery made it possible for one-piece cylindrical clay drainage pipes to be manufactured by the extrusion process. These porous drainage pipes were still referred to as tiles.

In the early 1870s the River Dee was diverted into an artificial channel, permitting reclamation of tidal islands. In 1878 the Seaton Brick & Tile Co. opened a new depot for business on the reclaimed ground. The company embarked on a programme of expansion. In 1878 it took over the works of the Esslemont Brick and Tile Company near Ellon in Aberdeenshire and also Dryleys Brick and Tile, and Pottery Works near Montrose.

The clay in the Seaton area eventually began to be worked out, requiring the Seaton Brick & Tile Co. to move to pastures new south of the River Dee in Torry in 1883.

In 1884 the Seaton Brick and Tile Company Limited was registered as a limited company. In 1885 a manufactory of agricultural field drainage tiles in Plaidy, near Turriff in Aberdeenshire, was taken over and expanded. Then, in 1889 the Northern Patent Brick and Tile Company Limited, also operating in Torry, was incorporated into the business. By the 1890s the company was operating five sites in the north-east of Scotland and was the only brickmaking business in Aberdeen.

In 1895 Alexander Christie, Junior became the new manager. In 1896 Ellis & Wilson began construction of a new head office and showroom for the Seaton Brick and Tile Company Limited on Market Street. This was to be a fine grey granite building. In Aberdeen, known as "The Granite City", red brick would never have been permitted, even for the head office of a brick company.

In view of the expiry of the lease at Torry and the near exhaustion of the clay there, the directors of the company put plans in motion for a move to a site north of Aberdeen. The new location was at Strabathie near to Blackdog in the parish of Belhelvie. The move would allow the business to construct a more modern factory and eventually dispense with the smaller establishments.

Alexander Christie planned the new works and Robert Gordon Wilson, a director of the brick company and partner in Ellis & Wilson, was the architect of the new buildings. Construction began in April 1898. An engine and 200-volt dynamo supplied electricity for machinery and lighting. Water was supplied

Robert Gordon Wilson was a director of the Seaton Brick and Tile Company Limited and was the architect of the new brickworks at Strabathie.

courtesy The Stone Trades Journal

from two sources, from the Blackdog Burn through a pipe fed by gravity to the engine condensers and also from a spring at Harehill Farm pumped by a windmill to a reservoir with a capacity of 9,000 gallons which was built on the side of the hill nearby. In the brickworks there was a 14 chamber Hoffmann continuous kiln situated at the west end of the complex. The easternmost block was the machinery wing. An office was located at the north side of the site next to the road.

The main machinery was supplied by Wootton Brothers of Coalville, near Leicester. The primary source of power was a 250 horsepower boiler 30 feet long by eight feet in diameter manufactured by Galloway of Manchester with a superheater supplied by McPhail & Simpson of Wakefield. A vertical compound boiler feed pump made by Green of Wakefield was fitted. A Green's economiser was installed. This was a patented device commonly installed in power plants. Its purpose was to save energy by utilising the heat escaping out of the chimney. Water passed through an array of tubes installed in the flue and was preheated before reaching the boiler.

Rowan of Belfast supplied twin condensing 130 horsepower horizontal steam engines each with a 22 inch cylinder and four feet stroke capable of working up to 250 I.H.P. The main shaft was driven from the engine by means of eight 2¼ inch manila ropes and power was transferred to the various machines in the works by patent belting.

The company also built houses for employees on the road next to the works. There was a three-storey block known as Seaton Cottages which was sited at the junction on the main Ellon road.* Twelve families lived here. A separate house for the works foreman was also built nearby. These homes were supplied by the reservoir fed by the windmill.

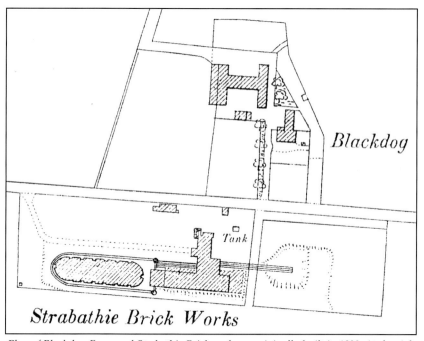

Plan of Blackdog Farm and Strabathie Brickworks as originally built in 1898. At the right is the clay pit connected to the machinery block by an endless chain. On the left is the Hoffmann kiln surrounded by rails and turntables. An office is sited alongside the road.
map created by the Author based on map by the Ordnance Survey, reproduced with kind permission

* These buildings were named Seaton Cottages when they were built in 1898, then they appear as Strabathie Cottages in the 1901 census. They are described again in later Ordnance Survey maps as Seaton Cottages. Today, they are known as Strabathie Cottages again.

In April 1898, the same month that construction started on the Strabathie works, the Seaton Brick and Tile Company Limited moved into the new offices at 182 Market Street in Aberdeen. The office block was shared with the Town and County Bank Limited, Market Street branch at number 180.

The new brickworks at Strabathie were inaugurated in August 1898 and by spring 1899 the first bricks were being delivered. Traditionally brickworks had only been able to produce bricks during the summer months. Provision was made at Strabathie for the production of bricks all year round by means of under-floor steam pipes drying the bricks. It was no idle boast when the works were described as having the most modern machinery and being the most up-to-date in the kingdom.

Seaton Cottages, now named Strabathie Cottages were built by the Seaton Brick & Tile Co. Ltd. to house employees. The block above was constructed of brick and consisted of twelve homes.
A. Gordon Pirie

Right: A separate house was built for the foreman at Strabathie.
A. Gordon Pirie

Chapter Two

A Railway is Planned

The finished bricks produced at Strabathie Brickworks were taken into Aberdeen by a steam traction engine owned by the Seaton Brick and Tile Company Limited. However, Aberdeen County Council was being over-zealous charging the company for damage to the road surface. The public also disliked these slow noisy road trains consisting of an engine plus two or three trailer wagons trundling along the granite setts known locally as "cassies" on the streets of Aberdeen. They were regarded as obnoxious and they really did frighten the horses.

Horse-drawn vehicles became the normal mode of transport for carrying bricks into Aberdeen, with traction engine when permitted, but the distance to the Bridge of Don was over three miles and into the city centre was over five miles. Alexander Christie proposed that the building of a tramway or a railway would make transport more efficient.

The city boundary at that time was the River Don so consultations involved Aberdeen Town Council and Aberdeen County Council. The Roads Sub-Committee of Aberdeen District Committee of Aberdeen County Council was the authority responsible for the roadway north of the bridge. The Seaton Brick and Tile Company Limited approached the committees above and the Tramways Committee of Aberdeen Town Council.

On 29th July, 1898 a deputation from the Seaton Brick and Tile Company Limited, consisting of Alexander Christie, and the directors Robert Gordon Wilson and John Morgan approached the Roads Sub-Committee of Aberdeen District Committee of Aberdeen County Council. The Chairman, William Bothwell of Berryhill Farm presided. The proposal was mooted that a light railway or steam tramway might be constructed from Aberdeen along the Ellon road to Newburgh. The meeting came to no definite finding other than the general opinion that such a service would be desirable.

Further informal and official approaches were made to the Tramways Committee of Aberdeen Town Council and to Aberdeen District Committee. By January 1899 again the general consensus of opinion was that the plan would indeed be advantageous. Among the advantages of utilising the public highway were that the route followed where the villages were sited already and less farmland would have to be purchased from landowners. It was estimated that with brick traffic from Strabathie, plus coal going to the works, the volume of goods would be at least 22,000 tons per annum. If the traffic continued along

The Bridge of Don, designed by John Smith and Thomas Telford, was constructed of dressed granite in 1827-30. The River Don formed the boundary between the City of Aberdeen to the right and Aberdeenshire on the left. The Seaton Brick and Tile Company Limited had hoped to make a connection with Aberdeen Corporation Tramways by means of this bridge. The narrowness of the bridge proved to be one obstacle too many however. It was widened decades later and opened in 1959 as a dual carriageway.

Author's collection

the tramways of Aberdeen Corporation much revenue could be earned by the city from the brickworks alone.

Actually, there was no great need for the Seaton Brick and Tile Company Limited to reach Newburgh. The aim was to have easy access to Aberdeen. We can appreciate though that the goals of the brick company and of the municipal authorities could more easily be attained by assisting each other. If the new railway were to be connected to the tramway network, it would not be too difficult for an extension to be built to Newburgh later.

Christie communicated with the managers of many other light railways in the British Isles. His aim was to ascertain if a similar type of railway could be built in the north-east of Scotland. His interest was aroused by operating practices prevalent in some of the Irish narrow-gauge systems whereby railway traffic and public vehicles shared the same road. The Clogher Valley Railway, Auchnacloy, in County Tyrone and also the Castlederg and Victoria Bridge Tramway were cited as successful examples of railways running on public highways.

It was not the first time that a railway line had been suggested with a route from Aberdeen going north via the coast. In 1845 The Aberdeen, Banff & Elgin Railway had proposed a route via Bridge of Don, Blackdog and Belhelvie as did the Aberdeen, Peterhead & Fraserburgh Railway in 1856. In 1898 the Great North of Scotland Railway also devised a scheme for a light railway to Newburgh via Bridge of Don with access via the 4 ft 8½ in. gauge city tramway lines to the harbour and the rest of the network. This plan also died though.

The local authorities were castigated by *The Daily Free Press* for not doing enough to assist the Seaton Brick and Tile Company Limited. William Bothwell, the chairman of the Roads Sub-Committee of Aberdeen District Committee, in defence replied:

> ...that the committee had been very favourable to the scheme, and that they looked upon it with considerable favour. Indeed, they had practically said to the company that they would certainly give them the road, and told them that they would put no obstruction in their way.

He was justified in making that statement since official minutes of committee meetings had intimated that all assistance should be given.

Eventually by February 1899 the Seaton Brick and Tile Company Limited decided to go it alone and build its own railway by a different route along the links over private land, thus avoiding the need for consultations with the various committees and sub-committees of Aberdeen Town Council and Aberdeen County Council. The railway was not planned to be a public railway, therefore neither a Light Railway Order according to the Light Railway Act of 1896 nor a formal Act of Parliament was necessary. However, it was planned that materials and techniques were to be used in order to satisfy the requirements of the Board of Trade so that their permission would more easily be obtained to carry passengers if the need arose in the future.

If statutory approval had been required, a formal or legal title would need to have been given to the railway. According to the local newspaper, *The Aberdeen Journal,* the line was to be known as "The Belhelvie Light Railway". Correspondence at the time also refers to "The Berryhill Light Railway" and "The Seaton Railway". In official valuation rolls of Aberdeen County Council, the railway is registered as "The Blackdog Light Railway." In Ordnance Survey maps it is named "The Strabathie Light Railway" which is also the title by which the Seaton Brick and Tile Company Limited called its railway.*

---

* The title "The Murcar Railway" would have been more commonly used after Murcar Golf Club took over ownership of the railway.

Arrangements were made with the landowners over whose land the line was intended to be built. All of them granted consent thereby alleviating delays and additional costs. Five properties were involved: the lands at Blackdog owned by the Society of Advocates and the estates of Balgownie, Scotstown, Seaton and Parkhill. The Society of Advocates' section was measured and valued according to whether it was arable land or wasteland which gave a figure for annual rent of £3 1s. 5d. The amounts for yearly rent payable to the other estates were consecutively £32 7s. 10d., £5 18s. 6d., £12 9s. and £5 8s.

Messrs Walker and Duncan, Civil Engineers, 3 Golden Square, Aberdeen were employed as consultants with James Watt supervising. Instead of having contractors do the labour, it was planned that the work would be carried out by brick workers under the supervision of Alexander Christie. This included laying the rails as well as doing the spadework. This would not necessitate having to take men off normal work, since operations in Torry were being reduced and actually made good use of men who could otherwise have been unemployed. It was not envisaged that any large or difficult engineering work would be

Bridge of Don Post Office and shop at the junction of Ellon Road and Links Road. The original plan was for a tramway to run along Ellon Road which runs from left to right on the photograph. The terminus of the Strabathie Light Railway was located behind the shed on the right on Links Road.   *courtesy Richard Stenlake*

necessary because the soil was of a sandy nature. The gauge chosen was three feet. No signalling system was to be installed since the railway was planned to be operated under the principle of "one engine in steam."

Walker and Duncan advertised for contractors to supply estimates for erecting post and wire fencing. A nearby resident, Alexander Hutcheon, of Cloverhill, Murcar got the contract. Fencing was for the western side only. Mostly the railway would be bordered on the west by farmland and on the east by links (undulating coastal sand dunes with rough grass and scrub). It was arranged that stone ballast be obtained from the nearby Findlay Farm.

The horse-drawn Aberdeen District Tramways system had been taken over by the city in 1898 and plans were being put in place by Aberdeen Corporation Tramways to convert the system to electric operation and to build some extensions to the network. The Seaton Brick and Tile Company Limited still wished to connect their railway to the tramways system and had high hopes of being allowed running powers over the tramlines along King Street. Alexander Christie was optimistic about a positive response and to this end designed dual-gauge wagons. This would have allowed wagons to run straight off the Strabathie Railway tracks onto the tramlines or onto the road without the necessity of having to transfer the goods onto carts. Aberdeen Town Councillor, Alexander Wilkie, Convenor of Aberdeen Corporation Tramways Committee supported the proposal.

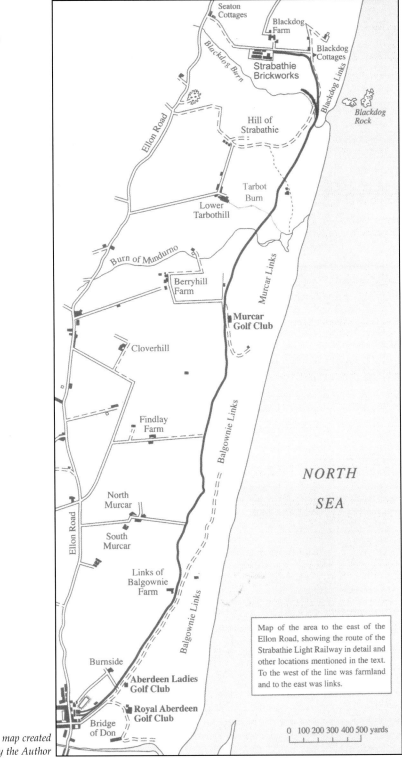

Seaton Cottages

Blackdog Farm

Blackdog Cottages

Strabathie Brickworks

Blackdog Links

Blackdog Burn

Blackdog Rock

Elton Road

Hill of Strabathie

Tarbot Burn

Lower Tarbothill

Burn of Mundurno

Murcar Links

Berryhill Farm

Murcar Golf Club

Cloverhill

Balgownie Links

Findlay Farm

NORTH

SEA

North Murcar

South Murcar

Links of Balgownie Farm

Ellon Road

Balgownie Links

Burnside

Map of the area to the east of the Ellon Road, showing the route of the Strabathie Light Railway in detail and other locations mentioned in the text. To the west of the line was farmland and to the east was links.

Aberdeen Ladies Golf Club

Royal Aberdeen Golf Club

Bridge of Don

0 100 200 300 400 500 yards

map created by the Author

Chapter Three

The Strabathie Light Railway is Built

In the third week of June 1899 construction of the railway began. Thirty-feet lengths of lightweight flat-bottom rail were used for the trackwork. Points and crossings were supplied in January 1900 and their construction was undertaken by William McKinnon & Co., Engineers, Aberdeen. The total length of the railway was three miles and five hundred yards. The steepest gradient was 1 in 30 and the sharpest curve was four chains (88 ft) radius.*

Members of the Aberdeen Corporation Tramway Committee and other guests were invited to make a visit on Thursday 6th July, 1899 and view the railway under construction. Firstly, the party visited the southern end of the line to view the area of the junction where the railway would join the tramway.

Then, just past Berryhill Farm a group of about a dozen workmen were observed engaged in construction work and the method of building up an embankment was seen. Railway wagons loaded with the sandy soil were run down to the end of the track. The sand was then shovelled into light "hurleys" or hand barrows and then canted over in charge of a couple of men to form the embankment. The line was constructed in short sections taking advantage of the slight downhill slopes thereby dispensing with the need for ponies to haul wagons. On the occasion of this visit the newspaper report specifically mentions *"The waggons are so made that they could run over the Aberdeen tramway system, in the event of an arrangement being come to with the corporation"*

The party of visitors were then given a guided tour of the brickworks by Alexander Christie and Robert Gordon Wilson. It was explained by them that the works were not in full production yet. Drainage pipes for agricultural purposes and tiles for flooring and roofing were also soon to be produced. These pipes and tiles would in future be dried in a drying-loft built on top of the kiln. It was in the top storey of this still empty building that the visitors were entertained and provided with luncheon supplied by Mr Stott of the Douglas Hotel in Aberdeen.

On 8th August, 1899 Christie made an official application by submitting a letter to Aberdeen Town Council requesting that they entertain the idea of making a connection with the railway. He stated that he expected the railway to be in full working order by November of

---

* One chain is a unit of measurement equivalent to 22 feet. The measuring tool used by surveyors was actually a metal chain.

the same year with considerable traffic. A Parliamentary Bill was lodged by Aberdeen Corporation for doubling of tramway track on some routes and extensions on some others. On Route No.6 a single-track extension was proposed from the King Street tram terminus over the Bridge of Don and 142 yards along Ellon Road to connect with the Strabathie Light Railway. Despite doubts expressed by some members, the recommendation was unanimously adopted by the Tramways Committee of Aberdeen Town Council in October 1899.

In November 1899 Aberdeen Town Council passed the motion in favour of the extension being built. This vote was not unanimous though, Mr Esslemont and Mr Gray were dissenting voices. Esslemont's contention was that this was not a light railway in the sense understood by the Light Railways Act, but a purely private line used for goods traffic only. Gray was concerned about the clearances available when constructing tramways in narrow streets. He stated that it was ridiculous to propose to lay a line across the Bridge of Don.*

Articles in the local press during November 1899 expressed differing views. *The Evening Express* wrote

> The action of the council is what might have been expected from a progressive body, for, as was pointed out at the meeting, the connecting of the tramway lines with light railways will add a deal of grist to the mill. The future success of the tramways undertaking depends on a comprehensive policy at the outset, and it is pleasing to know that the faith of the citizens in the Tramways Committee has not been misplaced.

The position adopted by the newspaper *Bon Accord* could not have been more contrasting. They were very much against the scheme and expressed the view that there was no advantage to be gained by the citizens and that the bargain was one-sided. The ratepayers would fund the extension but

> Few if any, will travel that way, and if we are to extend our line simply to allow heavy brick-laden trucks to be conveyed over our passenger lines, what is to be the recompense for the extension expenditure, and the heavy additional wear and tear that will be incurred? We are very suspicious indeed about this section of the Tramways Bill, and trust that the Council will see that under no circumstances whatever will power be given to these brick and tile people to make a profit at our expense, or to interfere in even the remotest degree with our municipal affairs.

---

* The Bridge of Don was not as wide as it is now. It was widened in 1959 to create a dual carriageway.

On 20th December, 1899 the Town Clerk passed a copy of the tramway bill to his counterpart, the County Clerk. There was no opposition at this stage and a detailed survey was made by a road surveyor. In January 1900 a meeting was held, with a resulting report by the district road surveyor stating that there should be no difficulty in making a connection provided that the railway line was laid along the west side of the bridge and not in the centre of the roadway thus preventing obstruction to ordinary traffic.

Some negative thoughts were voiced, for example that *"…one could see that there would be considerable risk attaching to the scheme, because the parapet was not a very high one, not more than three and a half feet, and there was no room for a restive horse."* Nevertheless, Aberdeen District Committee was of the opinion that the proposal should be agreed to upon certain conditions. Aberdeen Town Council should attend to paving the carriageway and installing lighting. Aberdeen District Committee should be relieved of all claims for damage and accidents during construction and while working in the future. It would also be a requirement that Aberdeen Town Council make a satisfactory bye-law to regulate the traffic.

Many local residents and users of the bridge were unhappy and voiced their opinions against any rails crossing the bridge. On 5th February, 1900 a meeting of the Roads Sub-Committee of Aberdeen District Committee was held. William Bothwell, the Chairman stated that while not wishing to put obstacles in the way of Aberdeen Town Council, the committee felt that the whole scheme was attendant with danger. They could not see their way to agree to the proposals as they stood at that time. The County Clerk was instructed, in communicating this decision to the Town Clerk to state that the District Committee would be prepared to consider any other proposals provided adequate precautions were taken for the safety of the public.

The newspaper *Bon Accord* was not displeased that this planned development was failing, as a disparaging article in the edition of 8th February, 1900 states:

We believe that the Aberdeen County Council did a good service to the city in refusing to be rushed into further consideration of the Strabathie connection with the Tramway system. In our opinion no party was to benefit by the scheme – at least to any great extent except the Seaton Brick Company. If ever the project is again taken up it will certainly be looked into with more care than was the present one. We can perfectly well understand Convener Wilkie's tears; but for our part we are heartily glad that the infinite amount of engineering has come to nought. The city has had a narrow escape - thanks mainly to the narrowness of the Bridge of Don. The line leading to the wilderness of Strabathie is not a light railway in the ordinary sense of the term; and it is not every car-load of passengers who would be so lavishly entertained as was the memorable party of City fathers and others who, headed by the Tramway Convener, enjoyed the hospitality-"full and running over"-of the Brick Co-and all for a reason perfectly well understood.

Towards the end of February 1900, the Roads Sub-Committee reported that allowing for a tramway line across the Bridge of Don; the margin was too small to allow sufficient passage for ordinary traffic. The proposal was attendant with several difficulties and could not be carried out without serious risk to the public. For these reasons plus the adverse feeling of people living in the neighbourhood the committee could not recommend the project to Aberdeen District Committee.

It was also becoming clear that there was not going to be enough time available for all submissions to be investigated by every committee. There was a fear that any further delays would jeopardise the whole Parliamentary Bill. Accordingly, Aberdeen Town Council instructed their Parliamentary agents that the Tramway No.6 extension proposal section should be withdrawn. This was later stated officially at the council meeting of 5th March, 1900. Consequently, the whole scheme was abandoned.

Once again, Aberdeen District Committee of Aberdeen County Council felt the need to defend themselves against accusations of dilatory and hostile conduct. Bothwell refuted such accusations stating that Aberdeen Town Council themselves had been lax, only informing them on 15th January, 1900 of the urgency of obtaining consent before the bill could be forwarded. As promoters of the Parliamentary Bill they ought to have known that more time was needed for consultations. Although it was being said in some quarters that they had interfered with a local industry, his feeling was that the Seaton Brick and Tile Company Limited would eventually monopolise the bridge to the detriment of normal traffic.

A four-wheeled saddle tank steam locomotive was shipped from the manufacturer Hudswell Clarke in Leeds on 29th November, 1899. It was named *NEWBURGH*, a possible reminder of the railway's future expansion schemes. W. G. Bagnall Ltd of Stafford supplied a batch of ten goods wagons in December 1899.

Although the planned link up of the Strabathie Light Railway with Aberdeen Corporation Tramways had been unsuccessful, the specifications for the rolling stock had already been submitted. The 3 ft

A drawing of Strabathie Brickworks in 1903. The steam locomotive with goods wagons is in the yard. *courtesy Aberdeen Daily Journal*

gauge locomotive and wagons were designed with axles arranged to suit 4 ft 8½ in. gauge if required. If the planned running of dual gauge locomotives and wagons had taken place the whole exercise would have been fraught with difficulties. The rolling stock could not operate on the Strabathie Railway with the wider 4 ft 8½ in. gauge wheels fitted at the same time because they would derail on the points and crossovers. One solution may have been to have removable 4 ft 8½ in. gauge wheels, being fitted when required to run along King Street. However, the 3 ft gauge wheels wagons still fitted on the same axle, though slightly raised above the level of the roadway, would have run the danger of fouling along King Street.

In February 1900 Aberdeen Corporation Tramways Committee received an offer from the Seaton Brick and Tile Company Limited to purchase four of their old horse-drawn tramcars. This offer was duly accepted and they were sold for a total price of £65. They were converted to the 3 ft narrow gauge used by the railway and used as carriages to carry the workers to and from the brickworks.

From Strabathie Brickworks the railway line headed in an easterly direction alongside the road through land leased from Blackdog Farm belonging to the Society of Advocates. The line curving sharply passed by Blackdog Cottages then headed south on a falling gradient past

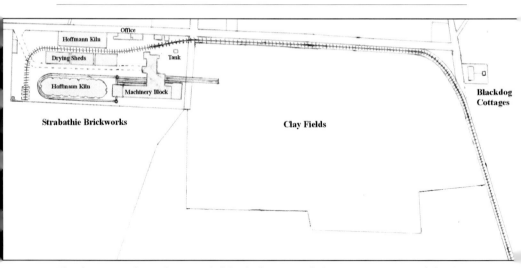

The above map shows the expanded Strabathie site with the maximum extent of the clay excavations and the route of the railway. A smaller twelve chamber kiln was built beside the road. Three drying sheds were built between the two kilns. One railway track at least passed between the kiln and drying sheds and curved round towards the larger kiln. A building of unknown purpose was believed to be located at the end of this track. Otherwise, the exact track layout and number of sidings within the works is unknown to the author.

map created by the Author

Passenger train travelling south past Blackdog Rock which can just be seen as the small grey triangle in the background to the right. The landscape here has changed because of high sand dunes which have built up over the years. The view dates from about 1904-1906.

courtesy John Alsop

Blackdog Rock towards the Blackdog Burn. At the northern end of the burn was a siding curving round to the west. The author surmises that loaded wagons were stabled here. The locomotive could drop off wagons from the works since it was limited to a train of five loaded wagons over the gradients further south.

The most difficult engineering work on the railway was where the Blackdog Burn was crossed. A 20 feet high embankment with a brick-built culvert was constructed to carry the line over the burn. At the southern end of the embankment a cutting 400 yards long with an average depth of six feet had to be constructed.

The line then continued on a rising gradient skirted round the Hill of Strabathie. This was 173 feet high and a very prominent landmark.* On the summit was what was often called "Strabathie Castle", a stone and lime oval shaped building with a conical roof thatched with heather. A point on the hill was an Ordnance Survey triangulation point and it was thought that the building was originally constructed to house a theodolite. The hut was later utilised as a shelter by the proprietor and family of Parkhill when bathing and shooting.

The route of the railway continued into the Parkhill estate through the farmland of Lower Tarbothill. Another two smaller brick culverts were built over the next streams to be encountered, the Tarbot Burn and the Burn of Mundurno.

The railway line proceeded through farmland at Berryhill Farm in the Seaton Estate. At this point a path led down to a salmon fisherman's bothy to which access had to be allowed. This was in addition to the usual access having to be maintained for farm tracks along the route of the railway. The line thereafter assumed a fairly level course by means of cuttings and some low embankments via lands of the Scotstown Estate.

The Balgownie Estate was next, where the line passed the fields of North Murcar Farm and South Murcar Farm to the west and Balgownie Links to the east. The railway line passed just yards by the farmhouse at Links of Balgownie Farm. From there the line ran alongside a rough track passing between Burnside Farm and the clubhouse of Aberdeen Ladies Golf Club. Aberdeen Golf Club played on Balgownie Links golf course with members of Aberdeen Ladies Golf Club playing on the nine-hole relief course next to their own clubhouse.** The coastguard

---

* Excavations and levelling off over the years have greatly reduced the height of the hill.

** Aberdeen Golf Club was given the Royal title in 1903.

The railway yard at Bridge of Don showing thousands of drainage pipes in front of the mill dam. At the extreme left, the locomotive and a whiff of steam can just be seen with the engine shed just to the right of it.   *courtesy George Mauchline*

station and rocket range lay to the east with cottages for salmon fishers and greenkeepers.

The railway passed Links Cottage and terminated in a yard at Damhead at the rear of the properties on Ellon Road. The yard was about a half acre in size and was used for stacking and storing bricks and tiles. The yard was paved with bricks. An engine shed, made of brick with an asbestos roof was built at the end of the northernmost siding. There was also an office and a store. The track layout at the Bridge of Don yard was very simple with three sidings and no run-around loop for the locomotive. Since the narrow-gauge wagons were comparatively lightweight, shunting could have been done using a combination of manpower and horsepower.

Adjoining the yard to the north was a dam which provided power to the Don Mills which lay between the Bridge of Balgownie and the Bridge of Don. It was actually more convenient for the Seaton Brick and Tile Company Limited to obtain a water supply from Aberdeen Town Council by means of making a connection with a water main which was already in place from Ellon Road to the clubhouse of Aberdeen Golf Club.

On completion of the Strabathie Light Railway the total construction costs including rolling stock were £5112 10s. 5d. This amount was well within the original estimate of between £5000 and £6000. The company now felt able to dispose of some road vehicles. A seven horsepower Fowler's traction engine and five waggons were advertised for sale at Torry in April 1900.

Sadly, Alexander Christie died on 24th May, 1900 at the age of 40 after a long illness. He did not live to see the fruits of his labours operating to their full potential. Christie was an enterprising individual and had certainly proved his worth as manager at Montrose, Torry and Strabathie where the business had prospered under his guidance. The brickworks at Strabathie planned by him was judged to be the best equipped of its kind at that time. He was replaced by Alexander Smith.

Alexander Smith became manager of the Seaton Brick and Tile Company Limited in 1900.

courtesy The British Clayworker

John Grant, Works Manager at Strabathie brickworks.

courtesy The British Clayworker

A view of Strabathie Brickworks circa 1905. On the right is the original 14 chamber Hoffmann kiln with two drying lofts on top. On the left is the smaller twelve chamber Hoffmann kiln equipped with a square section chimney. The chimney in the middle belongs to the engine house, to the right of which is the machinery block. In the centre of the photograph are three drying sheds for pipes. Bricks and drainage tiles are stacked in the foreground. The steam locomotive with its train of carriages is parked in the yard.

courtesy The Brick and Pottery Trades Journal

Workers at Strabathie Brickworks circa 1905. John Grant, the foreman is sitting in the second row, fourth from the left. *courtesy The British Clayworker*

Operations at Strabathie Brickworks

At the turn of the century large profits were being made by the Seaton Brick and Tile Company Limited. In Market Street more land was acquired to extend the yard. The Town & County Bank Limited and the Seaton Brick & Tile Co. Ltd. exchanged addresses, with the bank becoming number 182 and the brick company becoming number 180 Market Street.

In September 1903 a ceremony took place at the Strabathie brickworks to celebrate the silver wedding of Mr John Grant, the foreman, and his wife Elizabeth. The employees living in Aberdeen met at the Bridge of Don at 8.00 pm and were conveyed by special train to the works where they were joined by the workers from the works cottages. A programme of vocal and instrumental musical entertainment followed before the guests were transported home by train. This was just one example of the many occasions when all staff celebrated together with facilities provided by the company.

At Strabathie the clay-beds covered an area of 20 acres, eight of which were being actively worked by 1904. The excavations varied in depth from twelve to 25 feet along a face 350 yards in length. A second kiln, drying lofts and drying sheds were built. About a hundred men were employed in the works when in full production mode.

Letterhead of the Seaton Brick and Tile Company Limited dated 1906 showing an image of the head office. *courtesy University of Aberdeen*

The clay pit at Strabathie showing the clay being dug by squads of four men. The clay was hauled in tubs by an endless chain up a conveyor to the grinding mills.

courtesy The Brick and Pottery Trades Journal

The locomotive and a carriage were kindly put at the disposal of the police at Bridge of Don on Tuesday 14th March, 1905. An Inspector and a Constable had to make their way to Balmedie where the fishing boat *Excel* from Torry had been swamped with the unfortunate loss of all the crew. The train transported them as far as Blackdog Links and they continued by foot to the scene.

Positive steps were continually being taken to increase production and widen the choice of products available. The brickworks were now producing roof tiles, wall tiles, floor tiles, chimney cans, flower-pots, fancy fern baskets, horse mangers, cattle and pig troughs, sanitary ware and other earthenware. Lime, cement and sand were also sold. This was all in addition to different sized bricks, sand-lime bricks and drainage pipes.

When the brickworks was in full operation it attracted much interest. Members of the local press, dignitaries, customers and members of various societies were given guided tours of the facilities. August 1905 was a busy time for guided tours.

On the occasion of the visit made by about 80 members of the Aberdeen Mechanical Society on Saturday 5th August, 1905, the visitors were transported by train to the works and given a guided tour conducted by Robert Slessor, a director, Alexander Smith the manager, John Grant the works foreman and also by George Cassie, the blacksmith who had been involved in the building of the works and the railway. This guided tour had to be at a time when the works were not in full operation during the week so took place on Saturday. Half of the workforce kept working during the afternoon to continue operations for the benefit of the visitors.

Also, on Wednesday 9th August, 1905 a larger group of 140 people consisting of local businessmen, customers and friends made a visit. The train carrying visitors departed at one o'clock from Bridge of Don. As usual the party retired to a marquee for tea afterwards. On this occasion the visit was made on a Wednesday so the works were kept operating as normal but the workers were not ignored though as refreshments and entertainments were also organised for them.

The clay was soft and sandy and easily worked by hand. One squad of four men dug the clay using narrow-bladed spades. A second squad of four men filled it into six hundredweight capacity tubs or hutches. They were pushed on rails of two-feet gauge. The hutches were then hauled by an endless chain up an incline some 200 yards long to a 50 feet

At the claypit, clay-carrying wagons were man-handled on track of two feet gauge. The metal wagon at the bottom left has a V-shaped forked tongue into which a chain would locate to be hauled up the incline. This type as well as the wooden tipping wagon depicted above can be seen in the clay working photograph.   *courtesy The British Clayworker*

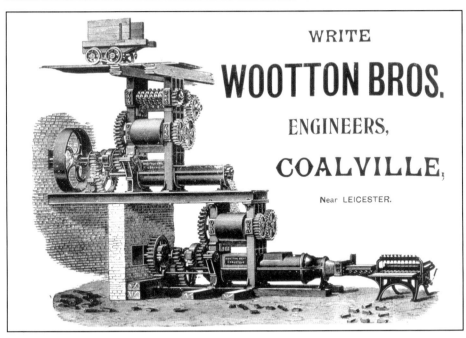

WRITE

WOOTTON BROS.

ENGINEERS,

COALVILLE,

Near LEICESTER.

The main machinery installed at Strabathie was supplied by Wootton Bros. The image above from an advertisement of the time shows the equipment used in the process from the clay being tipped in at the top, passing through various rollers and mixers and finally being cut into wet clay bricks.

courtesy The British Clayworker

The dryer at Strabathie was supplied by the Wolff Dryer Co. The bricks were loaded onto double deck cars holding 560 bricks each, then transported on rails with a gauge of 2 ft 8 in. to the drying chambers.

courtesy The British Clayworker

No. 5.

Double Deck Car,

FOR

WIRE CUT

AND

SEMI-PLASTIC.

No. 6.

SHOWING NO. 5

LOADED.

Write for Catalogues & Prices to

WOLFF DRYER CO.

14 Charterhouse Buildings, ALDERSGATE STREET, E.C.

Telegraphic Address—"EFFULGENCE, LONDON."

high platform at the top of the factory. One line took the loaded hutches up and the other line took the returning empties.

The contents of the hutches were dumped out 35 feet above the main floor level. In its descent the clay passed through a sequence of grinders, rollers and mixers which broke up stones and mixed the clay to an even consistency. The moist clay eventually passed to the pug-mill on the ground floor. The pug-mill was like a giant mincing machine in the form of a large iron barrel with one end tapering sharply.

Water would be added to attain the required consistency of clay. The pugging machinery was able to make hollow extrusions for pipes in addition to making bricks. The plastic clay was squeezed out of the pug-mill in a continuous rectangular ribbon three-feet long called the web. A die of the size chosen according to the size of brick being made was bolted to the end and a wooden mould was fitted to the die.

The clay web received a bath of oil to prevent it sticking as it passed over to the cutting machine. This was a table with a movable frame tightly strung with "piano wire" at the back. This was power operated with the frame passing through the web producing ten bricks at a time at the rate of 80 per minute. The cutting machine was capable of delivering at a rate of 3,500 to 4,000 bricks per hour.

The bricks made by this extrusion process were plain and smooth but the wires would give a rough appearance to the square edges. This was fine for common bricks suitable for inner walls but facing bricks for use on exterior walls would need to be re-pressed until they were of the desired density and of a smooth uniform shape. A press would also be used to give a special shape or moulded pattern. A frog or recess could be pressed into the top of the brick. A frog helped in bricklaying, economised on material and at the same time a brickmark showing the name of the manufacturer could be impressed into the mould.

Moulded clay bricks to be treated were taken direct to one of seven presses. There were two steam presses made by Fawcett of Leeds, one hand-screw press made by Wootten of Colville and four hand-lever presses made by Middleton of London. The simplest presses were mounted on trolleys which could be wheeled alongside the bricks. Hand-lever presses would be operated by one man who with a single motion of the lever would press each brick.

The bricks had to be thoroughly dry before being fired. This process was undertaken in a dryer manufactured by The Wolff Dryer Co. The bricks were placed on special double-deck cars capable of holding 560 bricks each and transported on rails with a gauge of 2 ft 8in. The drying-shed was 130 feet long, consisting of two tunnels each with four lines of rails. Underneath the rails was iron piping through which steam was forced. The heat increased as the cars passed through different chambers. The floor being perforated, the rising hot air passed up between the bricks carrying away the moisture which escaped up a chimney.

The final stage in creating the finished product was firing in a kiln. Rails completely encircled the kiln so cars could be stopped at any position required. The bricks could be lifted straight off the cars into the kiln. From the time that the bricks had left the cutting table to the time that they passed to the kilns to be dealt with by the kiln-setters or brick-setters they had not been touched by hand.

The bricks were stacked in a Hoffmann continuous kiln. The older larger kiln contained 14 chambers, each chamber capable of holding 16,000-17,000 bricks. The newer Hoffmann kiln was slightly smaller, having twelve chambers each holding 12,000 bricks. It was a long brick building with rounded ends and with walls more than five feet thick. Two parallel tunnels comprising the chambers ran the length of the building connected by rounded sections at each end. The kiln was divided into notional chambers since there was no physical division between them. Each chamber had an outlet flue to a central flue which ran to the chimney. On the outside of each chamber was a side entrance called a wicket and a damper to control the flow of air and gases to the main flue.

The unfired green bricks were loosely stacked in the chamber and then the opening known as the wicket was sealed. A fire would be started behind the wicket. The fuel of small coal was ladled from the top into the feed-holes which were metal pipes fitted with caps positioned about a yard apart. The coal burnt in the spaces between the bricks. Every 15 minutes the watchman removed each cap in turn and replenished the fuel using a small hand-scoop. A firing took about 24 hours when the temperature would rise to 1800-2000°F (1000-1100°C) with fuel, bricks and walls becoming white hot.

While the kiln was in operation the firing zone could be advanced in an anti-clockwise direction along the circuit of chambers by opening dampers ahead. Temporary paper divisions would separate each batch of bricks. The paper would burn when the fire approached. After one chamber had cooled the fired bricks could be removed and replaced by more unfired bricks. The waste heat from cooling chambers would help in drying and baking the green bricks being loaded into another chamber. Thus, the kiln could be kept in continuous operation as the fire progressed slowly around the tunnel, with bricks in the chambers being at different stages in the process; being stacked, drying, pre-heating, firing, cooling or being emptied.

Large quantities of agricultural field drain-tiles, drainage pipes and sewerage pipes in sizes from two inches to twelve inches were also made at Strabathie using power-operated machines and hand-operated machines. Two large and three small machines were employed making them. Two drying-lofts with adjustable wooden louvres were situated on top of the 14 chamber Hoffmann kiln each capable of drying and storing 60,000 to 80,000 pipes per week. Three separate drying-sheds were also used for pipes and they had a total capacity of about 30,000 to 40,000 pipes.

When there was a high demand the output of bricks and tiles could be brought up to 120,000 per week. In 1903 the works was quoted as being capable of an annual output of 5,000,000 bricks and 1,750,000 drainage pipes. This was at a time when only one works engine was in operation, the second being kept in reserve.

The produce was carried by train to the depot at Bridge of Don. The bricks, pipes and drainage tiles were stacked high in the yard. The products could be collected by customers or delivered.

Bricks being stacked by two brick-setters in a chamber of a kiln at Strabathie.
courtesy Aberdeen Press and Journal

The demand was seasonal, more bricks being required during the summer. Drainage tiles and pipes were stock-piled ready for landowners and farmers to purchase. Traditionally, field drainage took place after the harvest and throughout the winter period, particularly during February and March.

When off duty, the employees also enjoyed themselves together. During the summer, employees of local companies travelled on annual picnics and outings. Deeside and Speyside were favourite destinations with the Great North of Scotland Railway. On Saturday 1st July, 1905 for example, 50 employees of the Seaton Brick and Tile Company Limited went by GNSR train on an excursion to Speyside.

In common with brick and pottery workers all over Britain quoiting was a particular favourite at Strabathie. The game involved throwing quoits which were flattened iron rings weighing from 10 to 18 lbs at an upright peg set in a soft clay base. This can be easily explained by the fact that the equipment was easily made by the works blacksmith and the target area consisted of soft clay. As well as being an impromptu game played at break times there were many clubs in the Aberdeen area that played against each other at league level.

The Seaton Brick and Tile Benevolent Society held an annual concert and dance at the beginning of each year. The entertainments usually involved a lengthy musical programme. The 1905 meeting was notable for one contribution which was a song specially written for the occasion and performed by Dan Fraser, a popular comedian who was once employed by the company. (*see Appendix One*)

From 1906 Aberdeen Corporation Tramways provided a parcels delivery service. Small packages would be accepted for delivery by the tram conductor or at an agency along the route. The package would be carried by tram and a messenger boy would deliver it to the final address. The efficiency of the service was undermined somewhat whenever the destination was out along by the Strabathie Railway. It became quite notorious among the inspectors because the young messenger boys would take advantage of the remoteness of the area and finding plenty of other things to divert their attention, would forget to come straight back.

The Seaton Brick and Tile Company Limited had been able to pay the shareholders an annual dividend of ten per cent every single year since 1894. Unfortunately, in 1906 trade lessened and an unprecedented depression followed, especially in the building trade. Business started to recover slightly in 1909 but Strabathie Brickworks was only operating between May and October.

Chapter Five

The Murcar Links Golf Club, Limited

At the southern end of the Strabathie Light Railway, the track ran alongside Balgownie Links. This was the home to Royal Aberdeen Golf Club and Aberdeen Ladies Golf Club. On 4th December, 1908 a meeting was held at the Imperial Hotel in Aberdeen by promoters of a new golf club who wished to build a course on Murcar Links immediately north of the Royal Aberdeen's course.

Because the golf course would be somewhat inaccessible there was awareness from the outset that transport arrangements for members would be a problem. Even for members who had their own transport such as bicycles or cars, the road access was via Berryhill Farm, but William Bothwell, the tenant, was not amenable to vehicular traffic.

Since the inception of the scheme the club had been convinced that the best solution would be for them to make use of the Strabathie Light Railway. In February 1909 it was suggested by the golf club that for the first year, horse traction should be adopted with a return fare of threepence. Unfortunately, the Seaton Brick and Tile Company Limited absolutely refused to consider any such arrangement.

The golf club then approached the Great North of Scotland Railway (GNSR) suggesting that they might wish to operate an omnibus service from Castle Street to the end of Berryhill Road. The GNSR was very innovative with regard to bus services acting as feeders to their railway system. From April 1907 a scheduled bus had been run from Schoolhill station in Aberdeen to Newburgh via Bridge of Don and Blackdog. Initially they stated that they were prepared to run motor buses for the conveyance of golfers. Later, however, they became more cautious about the viability of this additional service, finally stating that they did not believe there would be sufficient traffic to sustain it.

The transit committee of the golf club consisted of members who were responsible for matters of transport to and from the course. Along with the club secretary William McHattie they continued negotiations with Daniel Mearns and William Bannochie, company directors and Alex Smith, the manager of the Seaton Brick and Tile Company Limited throughout March. These representatives returned to the brick company to see if some arrangement could be agreed upon. An offer was made to carry golfers on the railway at a cost of 7s. 6d. per double run but the company would not undertake the risk themselves.

On 29th March, 1909 the new golf club was registered under the joint stock companies as a limited liability company with the title of "The

Murcar Links Golf Club, Limited." On the same day, work started on the new golf course designed by Archie Simpson. The club committee members and persons involved in construction were transported to and from the course by the brickworks train. They were also treated to refreshments at Strabathie.

McHattie and members of the transit committee continued negotiations with Mearns, Bannochie and Smith throughout March and April. Eventually, permission was granted for the Murcar Links Golf Club to have running powers on the railway with certain conditions. The Seaton Brick and Tile Company Limited was to receive £100 clear a year from the golf club. The club had to make any alterations such as sidings and also anything which might be required by The Board of Trade. The golf club's vehicle had to be run at times which would not interfere with the brick company's traffic. The club had to accept all risk of accidents to passengers travelling by their own transport. The club also had to pay one quarter of the expense of maintaining the road from the Ellon turnpike road to the brick depot at Bridge of Don.

Finally, a settlement was arrived at with all parties agreeing to the terms being embodied in a formal agreement. The Board of Trade Railway Department had written to the golf club stating that as the railway was not constructed under statutory powers, the sole responsibility for its working rested with the promoters of the undertaking, in other words; The Seaton Brick and Tile Company Limited.

Murcar Links Golf Club had to provide their own vehicle, either petrol, electric or steam since the directors of the Seaton Brick and Tile Company Limited were not favourable towards horses being used. The provision of a locomotive and a separate carriage to accommodate 40 passengers was considered at first. It was then proposed that a petrol railcar be purchased which would run on a schedule connecting with every second tramcar arriving at the Bridge of Don terminus. The return fare was to be threepence which was expected to cover running costs. This would not pay for the purchase of the vehicle though and additional capital expenditure would be incurred.

The clubhouse was also being constructed with bedrooms for members wishing to stay for the weekend and also as holiday accommodation. In May 1909 the club captain, Robert Littlejohn, moved that the clubhouse be made of brick and be started on immediately now that agreement over running powers had been signed.

He approached Mr John B. Duff, Coachbuilders, Cycle and Motor Manufacturers, 460, 462, 464 George Street, Aberdeen about providing a railcar for the railway. Who said that he could build a 14 to 16 horsepower car for about £300 and would guarantee it for two years. Mr Duff was invited to come to a meeting where he showed his plans. After some discussion it was agreed that the railcar should be 20 horsepower at least and fitted with four cylinders. He was asked to prepare plans for such a vehicle and return with details to the club.

The golf course at Murcar was opened for play in fine weather on Saturday 5th June, 1909. Members and friends were transported to the course on this occasion either by motor car, bus hired by the club or by train. From early morning "a commodious motor 'bus" belonging to the Great North of Scotland Railway was hired for £3 3s. It ran between the tramway terminus at Bridge of Don and Berryhill.

Later in the day a train consisting of the brickworks locomotive and two carriages provided a service. The journey took seven minutes. Special arrangements had been made with the Board of Trade who, by means of a covering note for the day, sanctioned the use of the railway by

Members of the Murcar Links Golf Club and some Seaton Brick and Tile Company Limited staff posing in front of a marquee tent on the opening day, Saturday 5th June, 1909. Some people mentioned in the text are as follows: In the front row, second from the left is John Grant, brickworks foreman, next is John Thomson, Royal Hotel, club captain. Fifth from the left is John Smart, carrier & contractor. In the middle row on the far right is William McHattie, solicitor, club secretary. In the back row at the far right is a brickworks employee with a leather bag for cash and tickets. He was engaged as an attendant on the brickworks train carrying golfers in the afternoon.   *courtesy Murcar Links Golf Club*

visitors during the course of the day. No charge was made by the Seaton Brick and Tile Company Limited for the hire of the train, though a wage bill of £1 1s. 6d. for the driver, fireman and an attendant had to be paid. £5 insurance for the passengers also had to be paid by the golf club. Fares collected by bus amounted to £1 9s. 10d. and for the train £3 14s. 11d.

The train service was very popular so the Murcar Links Golf Club arranged with the brick company to continue the service every Saturday. The club provided a man to act as a train conductor. This was advertised as a regular feature until further notice. Golfers had to make their own arrangements during the rest of the week. It was hoped that the club would have its own vehicle built and running later in the year.

Although a railcar was not yet ready, members of the transit committee were making plans for the future. Proposed timetables had been formulated for weekdays and Saturdays. Sunday running was prohibited by the Seaton Brick and Tile Company Limited. It was recommended that the vehicle be locked in at the Bridge of Don terminus instead of at a siding at the club. The railcar could then run out to the clubhouse and return while the brickworks train was at the terminus. Then it would be locked up again while the brickworks train ran to Strabathie and back.

John B. Duff received the contract for building the railcar in August 1909. It was a four-wheel vehicle with a 20 horsepower petrol engine. There was a central compartment and an open coupe at each end for passengers. The club chairman arranged with Duff to close in one side of the vehicle and put sliding doors in the other side for an additional £5. The total cost of the vehicle was £356 10s. 6d. An initial payment of £115 13s. 4d. was made in September, with another two instalments to be paid in January and July 1910.

In November 1909 it was arranged that a wooden car-shed to house the railcar be built on a site north of the brick depot. The shed was constructed by Mr Simpson, a local joiner. Brick causewaying and a drain served to keep the shed dry. The Seaton Brick and Tile Company Limited offered to construct the points and siding and they subcontracted the work to Mr Cassie, Blacksmith, Bridge of Don. The total cost came to £43 7s. 5d.

A great deal of work required to be done in order to turn a smaller ladies' golf course into playable condition. Ground near to the railway had to be levelled and greens and tees constructed. Twenty men borrowed from the brickworks started the work at 7 am on Sunday 9th November, 1909. In addition to the manpower, John Grant, the brickworks foreman supplied barrows and shovels free of charge.

Chapter Six

First Railcar

The railcar service was inaugurated on 25th December, 1909 (a working day in Scotland until 1958) . The following report was presented by Mr Duff as to the running of the vehicle:

> The car was put on the rails on the 17th December 1909 and began to run in a regular service on Christmas Day, and has been running since according to the time-table (when weather has permitted), without an involuntary stop.
>
> The car was tested on 15th inst. for pulling power, and it pulled one the Seaton Brick & Tile Co's carriages with a total load of fifty-five passengers. This it did on the highest gear all the way, and as the low gear is double the power of the high, it could pull twice the above load if used on the lower gear.
>
> The car can also easily run up to the speed mentioned in the specification.
>
> The quantity of petrol required is about four gallons to four double journeys, or seven single journeys to the gallon. This is using Ross petrol at one shilling per gallon, including 3d per gallon of spirit tax. Lubricating oil will be about one shilling per week, 2/6 per gallon, and grease say one pound per week at 7d per pound. This gives a cost in all of about twopence per single journey.
>
> As the petrol duty may be recoverable at the rate of three pence per gallon, this would slightly reduce the cost of running, probably to the extent of about 4/6 per week.

The Club Captain remarked that *"J.B. Duff was a builder whose reputation was well known in Aberdeen being well known for the stability of his workmanship."* The railcar must have been eminently suitable though lacking frills. He added "that the car, although not an ornament, served their purpose admirably." Travelling by tram and railcar it was now possible to reach the clubhouse from the city centre within half an hour.

John Duff was busy training up a suitable driver. Allan Grant, the 17-year old youngest son of John Grant, the foreman of the brickworks, was on the car three weeks. At a meeting on 7th January, 1910 it was agreed that he should be engaged as the regular driver. He was at first offered a wage of £1 per week which he declined, finally accepting £1 5s. On 13th January it was officially confirmed that he would get the job.

In official club correspondence the railcar was usually referred to as an "autocar", "car" or sometimes "bus", "coach" or "motor coach" but locally the railcar was affectionately known as the "Murcar Buggy" or "Murcar Trainie". Less common titles were "Murcar Trolley" or "Murcar Carry".

More land on the west side of the railway was obtained from Tarbothill Farm in order that three more greens could be laid. Consequently, during the beginning of 1910 these extensions were made. The Seaton Brick and Tile Company Limited had to be consulted because golfers would be playing across the railway. There were no objections provided the golf club constructed two crossings at places selected by John Grant, the brickworks foreman.

A timetable was drawn up in consultation with John Grant. In January 1910 the timetables were posted in the clubhouse, at the brick depot, inside the railcar and posted to each member of the club. Before any more were printed, in March 1910, overtures were made to the Seaton Brick and Tile Company Limited to try and arrange a better train service. It was not possible to make a run at certain times of day when the brickworks trains had priority. The solution decided upon was for the railcar to be coupled onto the rear of the brickworks train, but until such time as couplings could be fitted on the club railcar, the brick company agreed to carry players on their train. This could only be permitted until 23rd April, 1910 when the works was due to reopen for the season between May and October. The arrangement did not please everybody though, John Duff, the builder of the railcar

A wooden carshed was constructed in 1909 to house the new Duff railcar. Behind the shed is the clubhouse of Aberdeen Ladies Golf Club. This photograph was taken in 1938 after Gordon Barracks had been built. The metal railings acted as a boundary.

courtesy George Mauchline

intimated that if the club's car were to be coupled up with a train belonging to the brick company, his guarantee for upkeep would be withdrawn.

During the first months of operation of the railcar, things did not run altogether smoothly. There were complaints about the car not starting punctually at the stated times, also that frequent timetable alterations had caused confusion or members had not been advised. A problem also existed because the last car was scheduled to depart an hour after sunset. Since sunset changed every day, this was a recipe for misunderstandings, resulting in golfers missing the last run home at night. To prevent a reoccurrence of this type of incident a bell was erected at the clubhouse which could be rung to warn members when the vehicle was to depart. An alarm bell was also fitted to the vehicle for safety reasons and warning notices were erected at various points on the railway.

Murcar Links Golf Club and the Seaton Brick and Tile Company Limited had an amicable working arrangement. The brick company even provided a shelter for golfers' bicycles at their Bridge of Don depot. In March 1910, however, the Seaton Brick and Tile Company Limited had occasion to write to the golf club with some complaints. Certain notices had still not been erected at both termini. The notices were to advise passengers were carried at their own risk and that the railway was not to be used as an access route to and from the golf course.

Another letter stated that factors from the Balgownie Estate had written to them reporting that the car shed had not yet been painted and requesting that it be painted at an early date. The proprietors of the Balgownie Estate also considered that the road from the main road to the entrance of the brickyard was in need of repair. The Seaton Brick and Tile Company Limited obtained estimates for the work, remitting details of the cheapest quote of 19 guineas to the Murcar Links Golf Club which was liable for a proportion of these cost.

Next month in April 1910 it was the golf club's turn to complain. Members were unhappy with the condition of the railway line. Strictly speaking, the lease did actually state that Murcar Links Golf Club had to accept the line as good and sufficient in all respects and was not entitled to call upon the Seaton Brick and Tile Company Limited to make any alterations or repairs. Nevertheless, the brick company was meantime making repairs. In the same month it was decided that smoking on the railcar should be prohibited and a notice to that effect was put up.

Playing golf on Sunday was a subject that aroused debate and public controversy and had been taking place unofficially on the Murcar course. In June 1910 a vote was held which resulted in a majority in favour of playing Sunday golf. No caddies were to be employed though, nor was the bar to be opened. However, the Seaton Brick and Tile Company Limited would still not give permission for the railway to be used for running the golf club railcar on Sundays.

The following local rules were instituted in October 1910 to take into account the hazards to play which could be caused by the railway:

(4) A ball played on to the railway at the 1st, 10th, 13th, 15th and 16th holes or on to the west of the railway at the 10th hole is to be considered out of bounds.

(5) A ball played on to the railway from the 11th tee must be lifted and dropped behind under penalty of one stroke.

In 1910 the railcar had to be booked in for its first engine service for two days in November or December. It was arranged with the Seaton Brick and Tile Company Limited that they attach a carriage to their train and stop at the clubhouse. Thereafter it became the usual procedure that the brick company would provide a covering service when the golf club railcar was unavailable. This would either be by attaching a carriage to a goods train or using the locomotive and one or two carriages. Since the brickworks was only operating during the summer months with fewer trains being run it could mean that the golf club could have sole use of the railway at times. The railcar returned to service in January after a thorough cleaning and overhaul.

A peculiar incident occurred on Saturday 18th March, 1911. It was reported that the golf club railcar was standing at the clubhouse when John Grant, the works manager of the brickworks, came up with his railway engine and pushed the railcar along to Strabathie without being attached to the engine and without the driver of the railcar getting the chance to take care of it. The club captain and the convenor of the transit committee spoke to Alex Smith, the general manager of the Seaton Brick and Tile Company Limited about the matter. A letter from the general manager and a letter from the works manager expressing regret at the incident were given to the club.

No reason was given for the above occurrence; maybe there was a misunderstanding about the timetable that day. Perhaps the club railcar was not scheduled to be there at that time, or on the other hand no brickworks railway movements were expected as the brickworks was not operating fully. Given that John Grant was the father of the railcar driver Allan Grant we could probably surmise that there was an element of mischief involved. When John Grant saw the vehicle in his path he carried on, either to teach his son a lesson or maybe just for pure devilment.

An interesting example of a joint operation was the shuttle service operated on Saturday 3rd June, 1911 for an exhibition match staged at Murcar Links between the golf professionals George Duncan and James Sherlock. As well as paying £1 10s. and agreeing to the usual conditions of relieving the brick company of liability, it was specifically stipulated that Murcar Links Golf Club supply the engine driver and fireman with their tea. The train service during the day consisted of the locomotive with one or two carriages, the railcar travelling alone and also the locomotive with two carriages and the railcar coupled to the train.

Grant the driver was dismissed later in the year and a new driver McRobb was engaged and commenced duty on Monday 28th August, 1911. Apparently, the railcar manufacturer John Duff was consulted since out of all the applications received, this was the only man he would agree to.

A continual programme of improvements and regular maintenance was undertaken on the golf course over the years. This required tons of horse manure, mould for top dressing, compost, topsoil, turf, grass seed, granite chips and even horse manure at five shillings a ton for a flower bed round the clubhouse. These materials all had to be delivered to the brick depot at Bridge of Don. From there it would be transported by train to the golf course in brick wagons.

In August 1911 a lot of work needed to be done to the course. Work commenced on a ditch crossing the ladies' course using 80 yards of twelve-inch second class pipes at two shillings per yard delivered on the course by the Seaton Brick and Tile Company Limited. New greens and tees to be made required a considerable quantity of mould. On this occasion the brick company were very busy and required all their wagons. Alex Smith, the manager, was anxious to oblige but stated that unless Murcar Links Golf Club could arrange that the carting contractor did not keep their wagons standing, the club could not have the use of them.

A number of breakdowns of the railcar occurred in September 1911, owing to over-oiling and subsequent clogging of some of the parts and the carburettor getting choked. It was recommended that the vehicle should be taken to be thoroughly overhauled at as early a date as possible and happened in November after the brickworks were closed down for the season after October. By this time Duff's guarantee had expired and future repairs would have to be done at club expense.

Petrol had been supplied by J.B. Duff. Enquiries were made and found that petrol could be bought direct in quantities of not less than 50 gallons and so in February 1912 it was decided to start buying direct at the lower price. The petrol had been kept in a store in a hole with a capacity of 60 gallons near the clubhouse. A more substantial petrol house was built two bricks thick which held the first shipment of 150 gallons. Unfortunately, Aberdeenshire Constabulary notified the club that they were still storing fuel against regulations. This meant that a special tank would need to be obtained for storage and the storehouse would need to be enlarged.

Severe gales were experienced in the Aberdeen area on Saturday 6th April, 1912. The golf club railcar was derailed and overturned by an accumulation of sand and dust blown onto the railway track. A passenger Mr A.M. Craig was slightly injured. The footboard and door were damaged and the engine was completely clogged with sand. This was an understandable and recurring problem since the railway ran through the links. Spark plugs were replaced and the damaged parts were repaired by J.B. Duff and Messrs Rae & Hunter, Carpenters, Bridge of Don, but the vehicle was out of action for a few days and unable to make the scheduled runs on the Monday.

The club secretary wrote to Mr Craig, expressing the club's sympathy with him in his accident. The following month a letter was received from Mr Craig's solicitors stating that Craig looked to the club to compensate him for the loss which he had sustained. In view of the terms of the rules it was unanimously agreed that the club would not admit liability. Concerns must have been voiced though.

Just at that time the insurance premium was due for renewal. The policy was with United London and Scottish Insurance Co. and covered third party risk. In June the club council tried to obtain an authoritative opinion upon the legal liability of the club with regard to the conveyance of members of the club and the general public upon the club's car, and if necessary, to cover their liability for insurance. The club secretary received a letter from George Davidson, manager of the Great North of Scotland Railway, stating that in his opinion the club was not responsible for any accidents to passengers in the railcar. In September the secretary wrote to the Royal Exchange Insurance Company informing them of this view of the club's liability with a view to getting a reduction in premium, and the insurance company agreed a two-year cover for £25, in effect a reduction in rate from £22 to £12 10s.

Bill McHardy recalls a tale told to him by his mother about how another accident was just avoided. Bill's grandfather was a farm labourer and for a few years the family lived at Burnside Farm, about a hundred yards from the railway line. One day in 1912 the driver came to the door carrying his two-year old son Sandy Petrie who had been sitting, playing quite happily between the rails, oblivious to the approaching railcar.

In May 1912, McRobb the driver made an application for an increase in wages which were raised to 22s. 6d. per week. After some problems with a leaking pump in May the railcar was running satisfactorily but a service was due. Arrangements were made with the Seaton Brick and Tile Company Limited to run a restricted service. When the railcar returned in November after an overhaul, McRobb had been dismissed and Smith, a more experienced man, had taken his place.

Considerable difficulty was experienced during November 1912 in maintaining the rail service owing to accidents, gearbox problems, and a broken connecting rod. A new model of carburettor had also been fitted to the golf club railcar for a trial. No sooner was the railcar repaired when the carburettor was frozen solid. More repairs were completed in December and the vehicle was running satisfactorily but consumption of fuel was more than it ought to be.

In February 1913 the driver Smith gave notice that he was going to emigrate to Canada. Another driver was engaged and was under Smith's supervision for three days. In March the new type of carburettor was still using more petrol than the original one so these trials were abandoned. An emergency meeting of the transit committee was held. It was reported that the engine was in an unsatisfactory condition and would cost £40 to put matters right as well as £7 10s. for a new carburettor. This was agreed to and the Seaton Brick and Tile Company Limited was asked to provide a covering service.

At a meeting on 18th April, 1913 the transit committee recommended that the driver be instructed to take not less than eight minutes for the journey, that not more than 36 passengers were to be carried at one time and the railcar must not leave the Bridge of Don terminus until the arrival of passengers by the Aberdeen Corporation Tramways tramcar scheduled to meet the club railcar.

The restrictions on road access had been a perennial problem. Murcar Links Golf Club was suffering inconvenience and loss.

Pedestrians only were permitted to use the Berryhill Farm road. When motor vehicles did appear William Bothwell would close the gates to all as a protest and letters of complaint would be addressed to the club. An article even appeared in the local press about taxi cabs being stopped and charged a levy for use of the road. This meant that rail transport was the sole means of travel for most members.

The railcar was a great asset to the golf club, but its purchase had made a big dent in the finances since the costs of a privately owned vehicle had not been taken into account in the original scheme. The heaviest burden on the club's finances was the transit arrangements. On average during this period the total outlays including rent, wages, fuel etc every month amounted to about £335 while the income came to only £235, a transit deficit of £100.

On the evening of Tuesday, 16th September, 1913 the railcar was returning empty to Murcar, when opposite the 13th green of the Balgownie course, there was an engine problem. The petrol ignited, the fuel tank exploded and the woodwork caught fire. The driver was unable to prevent the fire spreading and jumped clear. Within minutes the vehicle was engulfed in flames. Fortunately, there were no passengers and the driver escaped injury.

A satisfactory settlement was effected with the insurance company. A new body was built by T.C. Smith & Company, Limited, Automobile & Electrical Engineers, The Aberdeen Motor Garage, 21-25 Bon Accord Street, Aberdeen. Alexander Coutts of T. C. Smith designed the new vehicle. Club member William Yule was involved in the reconstruction supervised by Alexander Campbell the manager of the firm. A 24-horsepower Aster engine was fitted. The new vehicle was stated to be of superior design and workmanship* and commenced running on Christmas Day 1913.**

---

* The author has not seen any photographs of the original Duff railcar prior to the fire. The new railcar was described as a rebuild of the original and only the body was specifically noted as being new. Therefore, it is assumed that where possible, parts which survived the fire were retained. It is unknown to what extent the replacement body was similar to the original but the overall design concept appears to have been the same. Therefore, rather being regarded as a completely new vehicle, hereafter the vehicle will often be referred to as the "first railcar" or "older railcar".

** Christmas Day was a normal working day for most businesses and was not an official public holiday in Scotland until 1958. This explains why many events occur on 25th December.

Chapter Seven

The First World War and Murcar Wireless Station

After the start of the First World War in August 1914, trade at the Seaton Brick and Tile Company Limited decreased because of fewer contracts. It was realised that it would require a revival of the building trade before matters improved and that would not be until the war was over. Some additional income was obtained by letting unused office space in the head office building at 180 Market Street to small businesses.

During the war, wireless direction-finding was developed and proved to be effective in locating and tracking Zeppelins, German warships and U-boats in the North Sea. A network of direction-finding stations was sited along the east coast at Lerwick, Murcar, York, Flamborough Head, Lowestoft and Birchington. The positions of enemy vessels were determined by the intersection of lines of bearing taken from the different stations. The DF wireless stations were connected by telegraph wire with the Admiralty in London, so that after a German ship had made a wireless signal, its position could be laid down on a chart there.

What was perhaps the best kept secret of the war was the fact that enemy wireless transmissions were actually being deciphered. Unknown to the Germans, copies of their code books and signal books had fallen into allied hands. Intercepted transmissions were being deciphered by the code-breakers who were located in room 40 of the Old Building of the Admiralty in Whitehall, London. This branch of the Admiralty was a closely-guarded secret and known simply as "OB 40" or "Room 40".

Murcar Wireless Station was installed in 1915 with masts and wooden huts erected on Murcar Links and on land at Berryhill Farm. The station was staffed mainly by employees of Marconi's Wireless Telegraph Company Limited enrolled into the Royal Navy Volunteer Reserve, supported by Post Office telegraphists and soldiers to guard the facilities.

Obtaining suitable accommodation for the wireless personnel proved to be a problem. Negotiations took place with Murcar Links Golf Club but there was friction because the charges for unfurnished rooms demanded by the club were excessive. A note to Marconi's head office complained that *"This damned golf club is trying to make capital out of us."* Further correspondence was frosty but the proposals were modified and some rooms were eventually occupied from September 1915. The Club also provided meals and laundry facilities. Wireless station personnel were permitted to use the railcar.

On Saturday 10th January, 1916 an incident occurred when the brickworks steam locomotive running as a light engine ran into the club railcar. The railcar was badly damaged and a prominent member of the golf club was severely cut by broken glass.

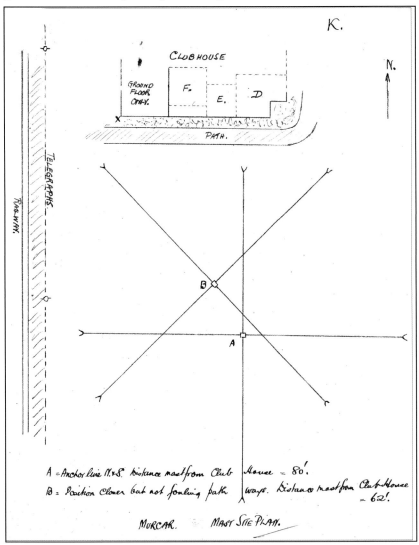

During the First World War, a wireless station was established on Murcar Links. The diagram above shows a mast site plan in relation to the clubhouse and the railway.

courtesy Bodleian Library, University of Oxford

As well as experiencing reduced sales, higher material and labour costs, the Seaton Brick and Tile Company Limited had been experiencing difficulty getting sufficient capable workers to run the brickworks continuously during the manufacturing season. Men who were members of the Territorial Army had been called up at the beginning of the war and many had left to volunteer for military service. The company continually advertised for labour, including female workers who answered the call to fill vacancies.

When conscription was introduced in 1916 the staff at the brickworks was almost completely dispersed by the army authorities and the major portion of the plant had to be left inoperative. As an example, before the war the brickworks office staff had consisted of a cashier, two men and a boy. By 1916 only the cashier and boy remained and then the cashier was called up. The Seaton Brick and Tile Company Limited reported a financial loss and no dividend was paid for that year. Many of the homes at Strabathie were left vacant or occupied by people not employed in the brick industry.

The engine which charged the large batteries at Murcar Wireless Station broke down in June 1916. Arrangements were made with the Seaton Brick and Tile Company Limited to charge the batteries at Strabathie brickworks. Unfortunately, towards the end of the process the brickworks engine failed. It was repaired but then the generator refused to operate correctly. This was due to dampness resulting from the brickworks not having fully operated for a year. Thereafter battery charging had to be carried out elsewhere.

Britain had been heavily dependent on food imports from the empire but Germany's U-boat campaign severely curtailed these supplies. By summer 1917 the situation was so bad that the government was advised that the country only had food stocks for a few weeks. All over Britain, War Agricultural Executive Committees had been formed to ensure that land was properly cultivated. Farmers were experiencing problems because of the lack of drainage pipes, due to the restricted output at brickworks owing to lack of labour.

In cooperation with the authorities dealing with conscription, during July 1917 between 20 and 30 men were made available to get Strabathie Brickworks going at maximum capacity again. These newly-acquired hands included men over military age, men who had been engaged in agricultural work and men discharged from the army.

The billeting arrangements for wireless personnel at the golf club continued to be unsatisfactory because of the cramped living quarters and excessive charges. Many personnel had moved into lodgings in Bridge of

Don and Aberdeen. In October 1917 though, when a new club committee had been formed, relationships between Murcar Links Golf Club and Murcar Wireless Station changed dramatically. New agreements were arrived at, including providing more rooms to accommodate unlimited numbers of men and better meals. A wealthy golf club member guaranteed the club against all losses. Saying *"As a patriotic man, I couldn't see boys walking and cycling seven miles daily in inclement weather."*

However, despite receiving income from the Admiralty, there was a considerably smaller membership during the war and the financial situation of the Murcar Links Golf Club Limited continued to deteriorate. Eventually the club held an extraordinary meeting on 14th December, 1917 where it was officially stated:

> *"That the company cannot, by reason of its liabilities, continue its business, and that it is advisable to wind up the same and accordingly, that the company be wound up voluntarily."*
>
> William McHattie, solicitor as liquidator signed on 27th December, 1917.

The following day, 28th December, 1917 was the first official day of possession by The Admiralty who intended to make more use of the clubhouse and parts of the golf course.

As part of the liquidation of Murcar Links Golf Club Limited the club railcar had to be taken out of service. The Seaton Brick and Tile Company Limited, using the locomotive and carriages, took over responsibilities for transporting wireless station personnel between Bridge of Don and the station at times suitable for their shifts.

Rubber ink stamp of Murcar Wireless Station, Bridge of Don Aberdeen.

courtesy Bodleian Library,
University of Oxford

Chapter Eight

Murcar Golf Club

A. Emslie Benzie, club captain from 1914 until 1919 and thereafter honorary president. It was thanks to his financial support that Murcar Golf Club was able to be formed so soon after Murcar Links Golf Club went into liquidation.

courtesy Murcar Links Golf Club

On Friday 29th March, 1918 a meeting was held to discuss reforming the golf club. The clubhouse was owned by the guarantors of the old club. The club was reborn with the title of "The Murcar Golf Club, Aberdeen". It would be dependent on the Seaton Brick and Tile Company Limited to provide transport. Insurance was arranged and a timetable was organised in April. Murcar Golf Club had to pay six shillings per week to the brick company for the extra hours of the driver on Saturdays. By the end of May a siding was being constructed near to the clubhouse. The Seaton Brick and Tile Company Limited supplied the rails, sleepers, points and fittings costing £16 4s. 10d. A wood-faced platform was erected on the east side. This now allowed the golf club railcar to be parked at the clubhouse while brickworks trains continued running.

In May 1918 the Admiralty took over more land and occupied the whole top floor of the clubhouse. A wooden staircase was erected on the outside of the clubhouse to provide a separate entrance for wireless staff and made the top floor more secure since it had been a common habit for golfers to wander around at will. By 1918 Murcar Wireless Station had grown to become the most important of the wireless stations along the east coast because it was not so prone to jamming. Many more aerials were erected and it had the largest complement of personnel with over 30 men. The armistice was signed on 11th November, 1918 but the wireless base was kept in operation.

Bridge of Don in 1924 showing the terminus with yard, sidings and engine shed. The "Motor Bus House" was the carshed for the railcar.

*map created by the Author based on map by the Ordnance Survey,
reproduced with kind permission*

The Seaton Brick and Tile Company Limited picked up coal from the Caledonian Railway goods yard on Guild Street, loaded into bags and transported to the yard at Bridge of Don. This could have been done by hiring carters or using the company's own horse-drawn vehicles. Carters were needed during the war when the company had a shortage of personnel; they were certainly hired in 1918. Some coal was dropped off at the engine shed, but most being transferred onto goods wagons and hauled north to the brickworks by train.

The brickworks train continued to provide transport for military personnel as well as golfers. In February 1919 the question of commencing to run the railcar was considered by the golf club. A trial run was made on the first Saturday in April 1919 to ascertain if the state of the permanent way was such that it would permit the vehicle being run. The railcar was now the personal property of club captain, A. Emslie Benzie. An agreement was made to the effect that the hire of the vehicle would be £1 per month for a year and that the club would pay for the upkeep and insurance.

By the end of April 1919 arrangements had been made for the running of the railcar according to a timetable incorporating Sunday running published in the newspaper. Thomas Sim was engaged as driver for a weekly wage of £3. The vehicle was insured with the Royal Exchange Insurance Company who covered against third party risk and any damage to Seaton Brick and Tile Company Limited property including the permanent way. The policy at first did not cover damage to the vehicle or compensation to injured passengers but this was rectified later.

The Seaton Brick and Tile Company Limited now paid Murcar Golf Club to take over the duty of transporting the wireless station personnel. The standard arrangement at the time was for the railcar to make a double run on six nights of the week for which 15 shillings per night was charged. About a third of the transit income was derived from this source resulting in a good balance of credit enabling the club to buy the railcar back off A. Emslie Benzie in December 1919.

In January 1920 an accident happened which resulted in damage to the footboard of the railcar and to the trackwork. The insurance company considered that the accident was due to wear and tear of the axle. Thomas Sim, the driver and others thought that it was in all probability caused by jolting on the rails which were not in good

Railcar with passengers at the Bridge of Don depot between 1919 and 1922.

courtesy Murcar Links Golf Club

condition. The vehicle was completely repaired but there were a number of items which needed addressing at the time. It was planned to overhaul the railcar during the next period of stormy weather which would prevent it from running.

In February 1920 it was decided that the number of passengers carried on the car should not exceed 35 at any time. The timetable was now being advertised free of charge in the local newspaper *The Aberdeen Free Press*.

It was advised that after 21st April, 1920 the special runs for wireless staff were no longer be required because the Admiralty were relinquishing the rooms. This did not happen as planned though and a new timetable was arranged for them. During July and August 1920 a new arrangement was entered into whereby the Seaton Brick and Tile Company Limited paid £6 per week to Murcar Golf Club for making a special run at 9.00 am and back in the morning and allowing the wireless staff to travel by the railcar during weekdays. Unfortunately, the brickworks train had to make some of the trips during August because of several railcar breakdowns.

Murcar Golf Club planned to buy back the clubhouse and to reoccupy the rooms and ground from the Admiralty who were beginning to overstay their welcome. The wireless personnel finally departed from the club's premises by the official surrender date of Tuesday 7th September, 1920.

The railcar needed a thorough overhaul in October 1920. Before that happened, Mr Trotter, the Bridge of Don Garage driver drove the vehicle for a week to allow Thomas Sim to have a week's holiday. The wages for the driver were now increased from £3 to £3 10s. per week. The brickworks train made the usual journeys for the golfers.

When the golf club railcar was next serviced in March 1921 some extra work was undertaken. The Kittybrewster Motor Works Limited, Automobile and Electrical Engineer, Powis Terrace, altered the transmission gear. In November 1921 the company noticed that the condenser and the magneto of the engine were giving trouble and rebuilt them for £2. They also built an improved braking system by taking off each brake separately, bringing it to the workshop and strengthening all parts with heavier metal.

1921 was the year in which the highest number of passengers, 31,746, was recorded travelling on the railway. Under the terms of the lease with the Seaton Brick and Tile Company Limited, Murcar Golf Club became liable for the building of a "bypass" road at the back of Berryhill Farm which had a new tenant in order that vehicles should not have to pass through the steadings of the farm. This work was carried out gradually.

In February 1922 the Kittybrewster Motor Works Ltd offered to overhaul the engine of the railcar, to be attended to before the busy season started, the work was duly done for £19 1s. 8d. It was agreed as suggested by the works that a new magneto should be obtained and fitted to allow the present one to be repaired.

A new iron panel for the railcar was obtained in September. New valves and a valve spindle were purchased and the valve seating was repaired. In order that maintenance could be carried out more efficiently in future, the club purchased a vice for £2 5s. which was fitted in the car shed, and a valve cutter and lifter.

In December 1922, when the vehicle was taken off for repairs, the Seaton Brick and Tile Company Limited train ran a covering service as usual. It appears that this was the last occasion when this convenient arrangement could be taken advantage of. Murcar Golf Club council was well aware that the railcar would eventually need replacing. In 1923 a car replacement fund was set up and £50 credited to it.

The railcar standing at the wooden platform beside the clubhouse of Murcar Golf Club during the late 1920s.   *courtesy Alan W. Brotchie*

This photograph is unusual since it was taken from behind the boundary fence and shows the side of the rebuilt vehicle which had no doors.   *courtesy Alan W. Brotchie*

Chapter Nine

The end of the Seaton Brick
and Tile Company Limited

There was a great deal of house building assisted by government subsidies in the years after the war. This demand for bricks reversed the fortunes of the Seaton Brick and Tile Company Limited which had been gradually declining. William Fraser took over as manager in 1920 and a dividend of 5 per cent was paid to shareholders for the first time since 1915.

However, the financial situation of the company was still deteriorating. Some repair work was required to be done to machinery and plant, and the kiln needed to be re-roofed. Profits were still being made fortunately and sufficient funds were available for this to be done during 1923 and 1924 thereby maintaining the works as a going concern and in a saleable condition.

Murcar Golf Club had been involved in negotiations to purchase the golf course grounds since 1922. At the beginning of 1923 the club also initiated communications with all the proprietors of the ground upon which the railway was constructed and with the Seaton Brick and Tile Company Limited with a view to obtaining permanent rights over the railway. The asking price of £2740 for the rails and sleepers suggested by the brick company was considered to be extortionate so negotiations ceased for a while. The club were reluctantly compelled to confine themselves to the purchase of the golf course itself which was completed by Whitsunday 1923.*

In January 1924 the railcar was involved in a collision involving a lorry belonging to Messrs Wisely Ltd. The railcar driver, Thomas Sim, maintained that the accident was the fault of the lorry driver, but the club had to pay the repair costs since the insurance company did not believe that they had a strong claim. When the next overhaul took place later that month, the brickworks train was no longer available to run a covering service so a charabanc was hired.

Murcar Golf Club had an agreement regarding wayleave over the railway which was no longer being used by the Seaton Brick and Tile Company Limited. In April 1924 the club was asked whether it was now prepared to take over the rails etc and the unexpired portion of the brick company's lease which would expire on Whitsunday 1928.

---

* Whitsunday on 28th May and Martinmas on 28th November were the two term days in Scotland when traditionally accounts were settled, rents paid and contracts were made.

There were two methods of procedure which the club was considering, the first of acquiring an option to purchase the ground and thereafter negotiating with the Seaton Brick and Tile Company Limited to purchase the rails, and the second of first purchasing the rails and thereafter getting an option to purchase the land. Mr G. P. Benzie of the London & North Eastern Railway gave a valuation of the rails which came to £792 1s. 9d.

In June 1924 C & P. H. Chalmers, Advocates, agents for the Seaton Brick and Tile Company Limited, approached Murcar Golf Club with regard to the purchase of the rails and were asked to name a figure which would be acceptable to them. The figure quoted was £2000 and again the council of Murcar Golf Club considered this to be out of the question. By this stage information had been obtained that there was every likelihood that the Seaton Brick and Tile Company Limited was going into liquidation and accordingly negotiations were delayed as there was little hope of coming to terms with the directors of the brick company at that time.

At the same time the transit council members of Murcar Golf Club made enquiries about the cost of an alternative scheme of purchasing a motor bus to run on the road which would enable them to come to a decision as to what offers should be made for the ground and the rails. With a capital outlay of £1230 for the purchase of the railway and the ground the total cost of running the railcar on the rails would be about £496. The purchase price of a 26 seat bus and of ground to provide passing places on the single track road to the clubhouse was estimated at £1160. The cost of running the bus on the road was estimated at £544 each year.

The only fatal accident recorded on the railway was in June 1924. The unfortunate victim was a chicken which got run over by the railcar. It belonged to Mrs Shepherd of Links Farm. The club decided not to admit liability but to make an ex-gratia payment of five shillings.

A special committee was formed by Murcar Golf Club and was authorised to endeavour to purchase the permanent way at a price not exceeding £500. They were also to try and purchase the ground belonging to the Balgownie Estate for £500 and the part belonging to the Scotstown Estate for £100.

The rumoured information about the demise of the Seaton Brick and Tile Company Limited was correct. An extraordinary meeting was convened and held in the Music Hall in Aberdeen on 16th July, 1924. At a subsequent meeting held at the same place on 1st August, 1924 a special resolution was confirmed: "That the company be wound up voluntarily". On 5th August, 1924 William Laird Clark of 222 Union Street, Aberdeen was appointed as the liquidator.

After the Seaton Brick and Tile Company Limited went into

liquidation it became evident that the liquidator attached great importance to obtaining relief from payment of the rent for the unexpired portion of the leases and from fulfilling the obligation to restore the ground under the leases. The northernmost section of the railway and ground upon which the works was sited belonging to the Society of Advocates was discharged by means of a purchase payment of £750 being made by the liquidator.

Murcar Golf Club made an offer of £500 for the land from Bridge of Don to the course boundary belonging to the Balgownie Land Trust Co. and £100 for the land from there belonging to the proprietor of Scotstown. If these offers were accepted then Murcar Golf Club would thereby relieve the liquidator of the Seaton Brick and Tile Company Limited outstanding rent and obligations, provided renunciations of the golf club leases were granted. Further negotiations took place and ultimately agreement was reached by November 1924 when the whole appurtenances of the permanent way were handed over. The ground upon which the railway was built was bought for the prices agreed. Also, the permanent way from north of Links Farm to the bridge over the Mundurno Burn was purchased for £150. The burn was half a mile north of the clubhouse so this meant that extra rails and sleepers were available for renewals.

Another view of the railcar standing at the platform. The roof-mounted radiator can be seen to advantage in this photograph.   *courtesy:Murcar Links Golf Club*

William Fraser, the manager of the Seaton Brick and Tile Company Limited attributed the eventual failure to the unfavourable location of the works, difficulties in excavating the clay, and the slackening of trade. Despite the building of the railway, the works was still a considerable distance from the nearest main line railway yard. Too much handling was required to get bricks to markets outwith the city. The greatest drawback, however, was the natural features of the Strabathie site. The depth of the clay pit was not sufficient to compensate for the extraordinary amount of sub-soil that had to be removed.

The brick depot at the Bridge of Don terminus was taken over by John Joss & Sons, General Carriers. The old brick engine shed was kept but new garaging was constructed. Mr Joss also had a new granite house "Tilquhillie" built on the site for himself and his son John Joss, junior.

William Laird Clark the liquidator died and Robert Gordon Wilson, of Westholm, Queens Road, Aberdeen was appointed as his replacement in February 1925. He was the original architect of the brickworks and was also still a director of the Seaton Brick and Tile Company Limited. Now, he was in the position of assisting and witnessing the dismantling of one of his own creations.

After the northernmost portion of the railway had been dismantled there were 70 lengths of rail lying beyond the Mundurno Burn which belonged to the Seaton Brick and Tile Company Limited. In June 1926 the liquidator was asked by Murcar Golf Club to have them removed. He advised the club that Clark & Chapman who had bought the rails had been approached and asked to remove them. In September though, the liquidator wrote to the club offering to give them to Murcar Golf Club free of charge. The offer was duly accepted.

Mr John Fraser, Auctioneer, Valuator, and Assessor 140 Union Street, Aberdeen held auctions during March 1927 to dispose of the brickworks and plant. The kilns and buildings were put up for sale as separate lots. Most machinery was in working condition and ranged from the large boilers and brick-making machines to small hand-vices. Railway equipment included wagons, rails and sleepers. Most of the brickworks was demolished in 1927. The former head office at 180 Market Street was taken over by Aberdeen Fish Trade Association.

The most visible evidence of the old brickworks was the 101 feet high chimney which remained in place as a prominent landmark until the afternoon of Wednesday 21st April, 1929 when it was demolished by members of 236 Highland Field Company, Royal Engineers (Aberdeen). A squad of sappers under the command of Major G.A. Mitchell spent several days on the exercise which served as ideal training in the use of explosives for the Territorial Army soldiers.

Chapter Ten

Murcar Golf Club's Private Railway

The previous arrangement whereby the golf club had exercised running powers over an industrial railway was unique. Now Murcar Golf Club was further distinguished by being the only golf club to have its own private railway. The length of the railway was 1¾ miles from the clubhouse to the terminus. The lifting of track to the north of the clubhouse gave the club the opportunity to expand the golf course.

In the beginning of 1925, Messrs Clark and Chapman, Contractors of 57 Charlotte Street, Aberdeen altered the track layout to provide a new terminus at the Bridge of Don at a cost of £111 13s. The platform was at road level with the track sunk two feet into the ground at this point. Mr Morgan, a railway surfaceman, was also engaged to repair the worst parts of the railway elsewhere. In February it was agreed that the railcar driver should have one Sunday per month free.

In March 1925, on examination of the railcar's gear box, it was found that two of the gear wheels were worn and that this justified renewing the two wheels to save further damage. Mr Frank W. Forbes, the transit convenor further reported that it was considered advisable to cover in the engine and the driving chain to prevent dust getting in and it was agreed to accept an estimate from Sidney S. Mutten & Co. of Catherine Street, Aberdeen for £7 7s. for this work. It was expected that the whole repair would be carried out and that the railcar would resume service after a few days. However, owing to a failure to get the gear wheels properly made, the railcar was off for over three weeks and a charabanc had to be hired from Campbell's Limited on most weekdays. From April two men were employed to repair the railway at a wage of £2

Frank W. Forbes, club captain between 1926 and 1928. He served as convenor of the transit committee between 1918 and 1938. During this period, he attended to the many repairs and upgrades to the railway.
courtesy Murcar Links Golf Club

per week. Rails were straightened, sleepers were renewed and weeding was done.

In June 1925 the driver Thomas Sim resigned. John Sutherland took over the duties commencing on Sunday 14th June, 1925 at the same wage of £3 10s. A new shelter at a price of £13 was ordered for the terminus at Bridge of Don and was erected in September. The vehicle was running better with a greater mileage being achieved after repairs undertaken during the year.

In December Sutherland was making enquiries about the timings during the winter period and it was confirmed that although the railcar would not be making a late scheduled run it should make a last run at dusk from the clubhouse to carry home workmen and also any members who had gone out by road. The financial accounts of 1925 showed a deficit in the transit account for the first time since the inception of the club. Interestingly the council of Murcar Golf Club wished to reduce the fares but were not yet in a position to do so.

In March 1926 the gear box of the railcar was repaired. A second-hand Argyll engine similar to the one already in use was purchased at a price of £12 which could be used when the original one was under repair. From April two men were again taken on to repair the rails.

During the period of the General Strike in May 1926 the question of curtailing the rail service was considered and power given to do so

Passengers, most of whom are female, clambering aboard the Murcar Trainie at the Bridge of Don terminus in 1929. The shelter erected in 1925 is behind the vehicle. John Sutherland is the driver standing on the left. The young lads may have been caddies boarding or were maybe just watching proceedings.

Courtesy Aberdeen Bon-Accord and Northern Pictorial

when necessary. When the driver Sutherland got married in June 1926 Sim took over the duty for a week.

In addition to carrying passengers the railcar was also used for other purposes and was run when the club steward took laundry baskets into town. In October 1926 it was agreed that a special journey would be made every Thursday for the club professional to purchase supplies.

Although the railway was provided ostensibly for the benefit of members of Murcar Golf Club, Balgownie golfers could also take advantage of the service, as Dorothy MacDonald of The Aberdeen Ladies Golf Club remembered from the period:

> How many times in my youth, have I sat in the shelter at the eleventh, caught in a rainstorm, waiting hopefully for the Murcar Buggy to pass. The man who drove it was a kindly soul and would never pass the 11th without looking to see if anyone wanted to be rescued. The fare was fourpence and we always kept some pennies in our bags in case we were caught in a storm.

Some of the passengers making the journey were not golfers but were just enjoying a trip along the Links in fine weather. Thelma Watt's friend, Annie, remembered that during the summer months she and her friend Katy used to walk up Links Road in time to catch the buggy up to Murcar and back to the Links later.

Complaints had been made about the railcar being driven too fast. In December, John Sutherland was interviewed about this and other matters. He was indeed unhappy and in December he put his request in writing for:

1. A new agreement with definite instructions.
2. Regular mealtimes including one clear hour for midday meal.
3. Half day each week with occasional Sunday off.
4. Curtailment of Sunday service to enable him to go to church.
5. Timetable fixed for the year regarding first and last runs according to light.

Unfortunately, the council of Murcar Golf Club decided not to agree to four of the five points. It was agreed to arrange a relief to drive for a half-day on each alternate Friday from 1.30 pm and once a month for the whole day on Sunday. One of the workmen on the course, James Gibb was later recruited for the position of relief driver in April and was to receive five shillings extra per week for the task.

In January 1927 it was planned to alter the platform at the golf club end of the line and reposition it a little further north to be in line with a path to the clubhouse. This was a wooden platform and was sited at the eastern side of the track. The railcar was off for a week in May in order

A view of the clubhouse from the east with the wooden stairs installed by the Admiralty visible. The railway platform was located at the other side of the building.

courtesy Murcar Links Golf Club

to get a new engine installed by J.B. Duff and the old engine repaired. The driver was given a gratuity of £1 for the extra night work involved. Two men were still working on the railway and were busy replacing deficient sleepers in June. In October it was reported that a new water tank was required for the railcar.

In October 1927 the council took the interesting decision to increase subscription charges for membership of Murcar Golf Club, at the same time reducing rail fares which were actually halved. It was the opinion of the council that no great hardship would thus be placed upon members because travelling to and fro by rail at the reduced fares during the year would save the cost of the increased subscription.

On 9th March, 1928 the car broke down but satisfactory repairs were carried out for which the driver was given ten shillings for his extra work. In April it was agreed to have all the bolts on the railway track tightened. During May 1928 the railcar was out of action for three days and it was necessary to hire a charabanc to make the usual runs while J.B. Duff attended to matters.

The railcar was taken off in March 1929 in order that the engine could be changed. A new tank was installed by Sidney S. Mutten & Co. A motor bus took the place of the rail service until the railcar was ready. In June a new sprocket and chain were ordered because the old ones were giving trouble. Some of the sleepers were being repaired and the railway was now in a much more satisfactory condition. Mr Copland, the blacksmith who had been working repairing the rails made an offer of £12 for about 100 old rails. This was not considered to be satisfactory, however, and the 80 to 90 rails immediately to hand were advertised for sale and were bought by Charles Brand of Dundee for £26.

John Sutherland resigned the situation of driver as of Saturday 9th November, 1929 and it was agreed to accept his resignation with regret. The new driver appointed was James Fiddes of Hill View, Bridge of Don with the same conditions and at a wage of £3 10s. per week.

From time to time Murcar Golf Club carried out repairs to the trackwork and equipment they had inherited. The work included weeding, replacing wooden sleepers, replacing rails, fitting steel tie rods to the track to bind the rails together, straightening rails and tightening loose bolts. Two men were regularly employed during the summer months on these duties and Copland, the local blacksmith was hired when repairs to the rails were required. By the summer of 1929 the railway was in a much more satisfactory condition but there were still some concerns and consequently it was arranged for a full survey to be carried out on Saturday, 9th November, 1929 by representatives of Messrs. Walker & Duncan, Civil Engineers, Aberdeen, who had been involved in the original construction in 1899.

They reported:

> We made our initial inspection of the line on the 9th Nov. when we had the Motor Coach at our disposal. The Coach did not run smoothly over the track and took some of the curves and turns with a decided jerk. A detailed examination of the worst places showed that the wheels were not bearing evenly on the rails, and further, that the wheel flanges were striking the fish-plate bolt nuts. The gauge (3 feet) of the line was found to be fairly correct throughout. The tie rods recently put in served a good purpose here and we could not see that spreading of rails had occurred to any extent.
>
> The sleepers in places are defective. This is most apparent in the cuttings where the damp is retained and tends to rot the sleepers. The majority however are wonderfully sound in heart.
>
> The present condition of the track seemed to us to arise from two causes, viz:-
> 1) Uneven settlement of the track whereby a list is given to the Coach on straight portions of the track, and the cant on the curves, especially at their entrances, not now being correct.
> 2) Waviness in certain portions of the straights.
>
> The roughness experienced in the running of the coach was accentuated by

the wheel flanges persistently striking the bolt nuts. This was due to the wheels having too deep flanges.

Before drawing out our report however, we deemed it advisable to get the opinion of a practical permanent way official. We obtained the services of one of the LMS permanent way inspectors.

On the day of the inspection, the less than perfect state of the equipment was confirmed when the front axle of the railcar broke and crashed through the floor. Unfortunately, a lady member, Miss Kilgour was injured. On examination of the axle it was found that it had crystallized. Two sets of wheels and axles had already been on order since the end of October with a delivery of one week but were not now expected to be dispatched until 21st November, 1929. There were two alternatives, to have a new axle made and fixed to the present wheels or to stop running the railcar until the new wheels arrived. It was decided in the circumstances not to run the vehicle. It was arranged with the Bydand Bus Company to run a bus between the Bridge of Don and the clubhouse as per the timetable. This cost the club £1 15s. per day for running Monday to Friday, £2 for Saturday and £1 for Sunday. The club extended their sympathy to Miss Kilgour and wished her a speedy recovery. Saturday 9th November, 1929 had certainly been an eventful day, with a railway inspection, a new driver and an accident. Jim Fiddes, the new driver was given work on the course until the railcar was back in service.

A second inspection was made on Sunday 1st December, 1929. This time the civil engineers were accompanied by the permanent way inspector from the London Midland & Scottish Railway Company. The report continued:

We might here state that the running of the Coach on this occasion was much easier and smoother than we found it previously, and we understand a new set of wheels had been fitted. The flanges were no longer striking the bolt nuts and it would appear that better fitting wheels and more adapted to the track had been secured.

After a careful examination of the track the Inspector came to the conclusion that the condition was on the whole wonderfully good and that it was possible to overcome the defects we have already referred to and put it in serviceable order for a good many years to come.

With regard to the way in which this could be achieved he gave it as his opinion that a couple of surfacemen could carry out the work of aligning and levelling the rails, packing up to give the proper cants and easing of the curve entrances, without much difficulty within a very short time. A certain quantity of sleepers would be required and the Inspector stated that second-hand ones could be obtained at 1/- each from the L.M.S Railway depot at

Craiginches. These are 9' 0" long and if cut in two would serve the purpose admirably for this line.

Of course we would point out that while the work now recommended to be carried out will give the Club a really serviceable railway for a good many years to come, too much must not be expected. It is an old line and short of relaying it completely at a large cost, it cannot possibly be put into first class order. All we say is that the line is possible of being put into such a condition that the Club can enjoy with comfort and safety the use of their Railway for quite a considerable time.

This, in our opinion, is an excellent suggestion and one that we would advise being carried out. For work of the character only experienced surfacemen with a practical knowledge of setting rails etc, can usefully be employed and we would therefore recommend to your Council that a couple of good surfacemen be employed to go carefully over the whole line from end to end and being supplied with the necessary number of sleepers for replacement purposes.

The cost of doing the work in this manner would be very moderate. It would not exceed, we think, £40.

In December Miss Kilgour made a claim for compensation in respect of the accident. Murcar Golf Club came to an arrangement to pay her £30 without admitting liability. At a meeting on 5th December, 1929 the golf club council considered the whole position of the transit facilities. The secretary got quotations from several bus companies for running at the present timetable. It was decided that unless any change in the mode of transit was demanded at the annual general meeting, then Messrs Walker and Duncan would be instructed to carry out repairs as suggested by them.

The repair work was agreed to in January 1930. The club purchased the wooden sleepers from the LMS and two railway surfacemen, George Campbell and John George were hired to remedy the faults. Over a period of four weeks in January and February in 1930, sleepers were replaced and the track was levelled and realigned for a total cost of £47 18s. 3d. which included labour as well as materials.

Messrs Walker & Duncan finally suggested that:

The Railway, having been brought to a serviceable state, we would suggest that, to keep it so, it would be to the club's advantage to have it gone over say once every year or so by these surfacemen, so that any small defect developing in the level or the alignment of the rails could be rectified at small cost. Not only would the life of the railway be extended but the wear and tear on the motor coach would be kept down.

Murcar Golf Club expressed its satisfaction on the manner in which the problems had been approached and the work completed. The club also promised to keep their recommendations in mind.

At the end of April 1930 owing to a defect in the main drive to the gear box the railcar broke down and five of the staff had to push it to the depot. They were given two shillings each for their trouble. The car was taken off for three days and a bus was hired for that time. It was decided to purchase a new chain and sprocket and to have them fitted as soon as possible. The following month the vehicle was off sick again. A new driving shaft was obtained and a new axle brake was being fixed up. In June the difficulty of getting the railcar repaired when it went wrong was considered and it was ultimately agreed that after these repairs were carried out by George Cassie, Engineers, to employ in future John Joss, Motor Engineer, Bridge of Don whose premises were sited in the former brick depot.

In September 1930 Joss was asked to give a detailed report on the condition of the engine. This was planned while the driver was given a holiday on the first week in October. It had not been a good year for the railcar so far. It was not a good year for the unfortunate Miss Kilgour either, who suffered yet another injury. The sliding door came off its rail and fell on her head. New replacement rollers and a rail for the door were obtained. It is not recorded whether Miss Kilgour continued as a member of the club or found alternative means of transport!

In consequence of a broken beam which supported the engine it was necessary to take the railcar off for repairs for a fortnight in November 1930. At the same time an inspection and overhaul were undertaken. John Joss gave his opinion that the engine as repaired would give a good spell of service, but the doors, the wooden beams and framing would all have to be repaired. The club council decided to have the doors properly repaired forthwith but to do nothing further in regard to the wooden beams and framing meantime.

Joss reported that a contributory factor to some of the recent problems had been overloading. The driver was instructed to carry only 32 at a time as otherwise the strain might be too much for the vehicle. In any case this was the number of passengers permitted by the terms of the insurance policy. A reminder notice to this effect was posted inside the vehicle and in the clubhouse. At the annual general meeting of 1930 the council of Murcar Golf Club were of the opinion that in the near future the purchase of a new railcar must be faced. If a new vehicle were obtained, then the older one could be kept in reserve for emergencies, and save on very heavy charges for hire of buses when repairs were required.

Chapter Eleven

Second Railcar

Specifications for a new railcar were drawn up and sent to three engineering companies. By February 1931 an estimate had been received from Messrs D. Wickham & Company Ltd, Ware, Hertfordshire, offering to supply a railcar for £1200. Another offer was received from Messrs J. & H. McLaren Ltd, Leeds. As these estimates ranged from £1000 to £1200 Murcar Golf Club Council decided to considerably modify the specifications and that nothing should be decided yet.

A representative of Wickham & Co. inspected the club's old railcar and suggested an arrangement might be possible whereby they would supply a chassis, the body to be built in Aberdeen. In April an offer from Wickham to build a chassis and all other parts for a new vehicle with the exception of the body for £350 was submitted. The council were not satisfied that this was the lowest price at which a chassis could be obtained so enquiries were made with Mr W. F. Scott of Aberdeen

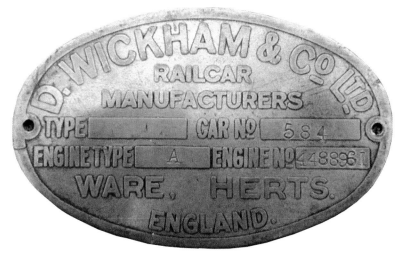

Maker's works plate from the Wickham railcar. These were officially known by the manufacturer as "Wickham name plates." It is a standard shape measuring 2½ inches x 4 inches and made of brass. Only one plate was supplied for each vehicle built by the company, the details added by being cold stamped. The TYPE is left blank since the vehicle supplied to Murcar Golf Club was a one-off and not a standard type. It is described as "As Drawing No.906/A." CAR No. 584 was a sequential number allocated to every vehicle manufactured by the company. ENGINE TYPE and ENGINE No. shows that the engine fitted was a Ford type "A" with the serial number 4488961.

courtesy Aberdeen Transport Society

Motors and also with the Leyland agents in Aberdeen. Mr Scott of Aberdeen Motors procured an estimate of £413 from J.M. Henderson of Aberdeen. The local firm's estimates being dearer, the club reverted to Wickham and Company Ltd.

A special notice was put up in the clubhouse in May 1931 to remind members that when the railcar broke down, they should make use of the public buses on the main road between Aberdeen and Ellon. This was maybe a premonition or more likely just a reflection on the confidence in the railcar and track. Walker and Duncan, civil engineers, had already been instructed to overhaul the permanent way. For two weeks during May and June in 1931 the two surfacemen, George Campbell and John George, were again hard at work doing maintenance including cutting whin* bushes, repairing and levelling track and laying new sleepers. Their services were timely because sure enough when the vehicle was running towards the clubhouse it jumped off the rails. Considerable damage was done and the costs had to be reclaimed through the insurance policy. The driver was given an additional ten shillings for the extra work involved in carrying out repairs.

An unusual alternative transit scheme was costed in November 1931 by Mr William Walker, Ashgrove Motor Works, Ashgrove Road, Aberdeen. He recommended that the permanent way of the railway could be converted into a road on which a motor bus costing £855 could be run. The council of Murcar Golf Club, however, considered that the initial cost of converting the railway into a road was out of the question.

In January 1932 estimates for a body for the new railcar were obtained. Messrs J. Shepherd & Sons, Wheelwrights & Commercial Motor Vehicle Builders, 61 John Street quoted £250. Messrs J. & J. Ingram, Cartwright & Motor Body Builders, 72 Hutcheon Street quoted £180. As no reply to another letter asking for a quotation for a complete vehicle had been received from Wickham & Co., it was decided to defer further consideration until their estimate was received.

Then in February, Messrs D. Wickham & Company Ltd submitted an offer to supply a railcar at a price of £600 delivered at the club's depot at Bridge of Don. The transit committee suggested some alterations be made and the offer was accepted. It was a four-wheel vehicle of 24 horsepower, a totally enclosed design with driving controls at both ends. The driver's cab was at one end which held the engine and seating for five passengers. There was a main passenger compartment with seating for 35.

---

* Whins: *Ulex europaeus*, the common furze or gorse

William C. Smith, one of the staff on the golf course, was given the job of relief driver in May 1932. He was paid £2 5s. per week of which five shillings was for driving the railcar. That month a shed to house the new railcar was built at a cost of £114 15s. 6d. Measuring 36 ft x 13 ft it was constructed of corrugated-iron and was sited at Bridge of Don beside the shelter on Links Road. There was a pit inside to assist the driver in oiling the engine and other maintenance work.

The new Wickham railcar was duly delivered on 11th July, 1932. The "launching" onto the tracks was accomplished by Messrs James Abernethy & Co. Ltd, Ferryhill Foundry, Aberdeen. It was described at the time as a more roomy, better built and better sprung vehicle. Unfortunately, it did not conform in several ways to the specifications. It was reported that after considerable trouble there still remained certain things to be attended to. Messrs Joss & Sons stated that the roof was satisfactory after two coats of white lead paint had been applied. A payment of just £450 was made to Wickham & Co. meantime and the makers were called upon to remedy the defects at their expense. Mr MacIntosh, painter was given the job of painting on the vehicle and clubhouse doors a sign stating "Private for Members and Players only."

This corrugated-iron carshed was built at the end of the line on Links Road specially to house the new Wickham railcar. The photograph was taken at the end of its life.

A. Gordon Pirie

The Wickham railcar parked outside the shed. This view shows the front and right-hand side.
photograph by H.R. MacKenzie, courtesy of The Railway Magazine

On Friday 7th October, 1932 it was reported that the railcar was not working satisfactorily. The six months maintenance guarantee was actually to start from this date. It was decided that part of the payment to the manufacturer would be withheld until April. Other improvements were now attended to.

At the beginning of 1933 some parts of the new railcar still failed to give satisfaction. Messrs Wickham & Co. accepted responsibility for certain valves which had worn out. When the guarantee expired in April, Joss inspected the vehicle and could find no further fault. The balance of payment was made to the manufacturer after deducting the price of alterations which had to be done locally.

The sleepers underneath the sets of points at the depot had been replaced already, and in the summer of 1933 a full overhaul of the permanent way was undertaken. Three hundred wooden sleepers were bought in May with a view to replacing all the sleepers on the railway during the course of the next five years. It was expected that in the future, annual expenditure on maintenance would be considerably reduced. The work resulted in a large number of old sleepers being made available for sale.

One of the redundant sleepers was put to good use as a removable barrier in front of the car shed. The sleeper was laid across the rails near the entrance to the shed and kept in position by two pins set into the ground at either side. This was done after an incident in October 1933 when the brakes of the older railcar failed resulting in damage to the new car shed. Repairs were done to the car by John Joss & Sons and to the shed by Messrs D. MacAndrew & Co. Ltd., Builders & Contractors, 120 Loch Street, Aberdeen. Instructions were given to the driver not to go so fast, not to accelerate on bends and to switch the engine off if at any time the brakes should not work.

On Thursday 21st December, 1933 an alteration was made to Murcar Golf Club rules governing transit facilities.

> 3. Rule 44 shall be deleted and the following rule submitted therefore viz:- Members and others travelling by rail to and from the Clubhouse by the club's car or any other vehicle owned, hired or used by the club shall do so at their own risk, and they or their representatives shall have no claims against the club or its officials in respect of injury or loss resulting from accident or any other cause.

During the spring and summer of 1934, the sleepers at all curves were turned and re-gauged where this had not already been carried out. It was agreed that no new sleepers be purchased for the time being. The permanent way was also cleaned. Repairs were made to the shelter at Bridge of Don and the wooden car shed was also repaired and tarred.

In 1935 the convenor of the transit committee consulted with Messrs John Joss & Sons about having periodical examinations done and also investigated any other ways in which the transit expenses could be reduced. The driver was asked to try and reduce the number of trips wherever possible. In February it was arranged to have regular three-monthly inspections of the vehicle done by John Joss. A reconditioned 24 horsepower Ford engine was purchased for £26 10s. in May and installed in the Wickham railcar. The old engine was to be repaired and kept as a spare in Joss's yard. Two windows of the new car shed were reported broken so all the windows were replaced by wood.

In the summer of 1935, some track repairs were required but the club had difficulty in getting a surfaceman to do the work. In the meantime, all that could be done was scything the grass with a supervisor supplied by William Tawse, Contractor. It was not until late November that the club got Mr Watt, a surfaceman and Mr Ewen who would undertake the overhaul of the permanent way but even then, they couldn't do so immediately. Some club members who didn't travel by the railcar sportingly contributed "voluntary fares" to assist with the upkeep of the railway.

Gerald Joss remembers that his father Jack along with Bertie Fiddes (the brother of driver Jim Fiddes) often had to tramp up the line, tools at the ready, to make repairs and it would often be to the newer Wickham railcar, the older vehicle proving more reliable at this particular time. In

April 1936 a 300 gallon petrol tank was installed near to the clubhouse by Alexander Cheyne Limited, Motor and Cycle Factors, 8 Union Row, Aberdeen. The costs of £26 6s. 3d. included excavating a pit and fitting a second-hand pump and piping. Bulk purchases of petrol would in future mean a saving for the club. The steward was to keep the key and the driver and head greenkeeper were to keep a record of petrol drawn from the tank.

Railway employees Alexander Anderson and George Sherriffs worked on the maintenance when 100 new sleepers were bought in 1936 and were paid one shilling an hour and £2 5s. per week respectively, both working a nine hour day. Gravel was put down as ballast and Murcar Golf Club was assured that it would be many years before anything further in the way of ballast was required. When that work had been completed in June, they were engaged in making an alteration on the platform at the clubhouse and levelling the ground west of the railcar stance.

At the clubhouse the bell was rung from five to ten minutes before departure to allow golfers and caddies at the 18th hole sufficient time to catch the train. A later departure could also be guaranteed as J. I. McGee of Murcar Golf Club remembers: *"older members recall with nostalgia the old buggy and its indomitable driver, Jimmy Fiddes, who could always be persuaded to delay the last run by the promise of a dram."*

Unfortunately, Jim Fiddes could overdo it at times. In June 1936 Murcar Golf Club Council decided to terminate his services, as he had been the worse for wear on a particular Wednesday. A letter of apology was submitted by him and in the circumstances the council agreed to re-instate him.

Terms and conditions of employment for position of driver were made clear.

1. That his wages would be £3 10s. during the months of April to September inclusive and during the other months £2 10s.
2. That on no account must he touch liquor during his runs and that if he showed any sign of liquor while on duty he would be dismissed without warning.
3. That he must keep the car stance at the clubhouse and at the depot at the Bridge of Don in a tidy condition.
4. That he must drive the car carefully as speeding was detrimental not only to the rails but to the car itself.
5. That he must wear while on duty a driver's cap to be supplied at the club's expense.

The appearance of the Bridge of Don area had changed considerably between 1932 and 1935 when the Gordon Barracks was built. The formal opening was on 14th September, 1935 and this became the new depot for the Gordon Highlanders whose home had previously been Castlehill Barracks in Aberdeen. Some small disputes occurred regarding access to cut grass and a level crossing built by the army without permission over the railway. All matters were settled amicably, with the club reminding them that any movement around the railway was at their own risk.

A railcar body (it's unclear which railcar) was painted by Kenneth Mackintosh, Painter & Decorator, 20 Loch Street, Aberdeen for £6 6s. 6d.* From October the driver was to receive £3 per week instead of the previous pay scale of £3 10s. during the six summer months and £2 10s. during the winter months.

In 1937 Bill Tough's family moved into Links Farm where the railway ran just yards past the buildings. Bill recalls Jim Fiddes giving a loud warning shout as he drove the railcar through the farm and there would be a flurry of fur and feathers as the cats and chickens dodged out of the way. Jim was happy to provide an unofficial public transport service to the farming families who lived along the route of the railway. This was handy when provisions had to be carried from the Bridge of Don and could be critical in winter when the road would often be blocked by snow but the railway line would still be clear.

In January 1938 alterations to the timetable were considered with a view to reducing the number of runs thereby saving costs. The grass and weeds proliferating on the railway were cleared during the summer of 1938 for which Mr James Milne and an assistant were hired at wages of 1s. 2d. and 1s. respectively for a 48 hour week. The curves had to be adjusted and some new wooden sleepers laid. In late September the Wickham railcar was off for three days owing to a defect in a rocking bearer in an axle. The engine was also replaced with the spare one.

In October it was discovered that a roll of tickets had been stolen from the railcar. It appeared that the loss had actually occurred in August but Fiddes had not reported the matter, perhaps concerned for his personal position and had paid the £1 6d. out of his own pocket. The money was repaid to him with a censure to notify any discrepancies in the future.

Harold (Bud) Bishop worked as a caddy from the age of ten at Royal Aberdeen Golf Club from 1928 to 1938. When there was no work available at the Balgownie course the caddies travelled up to the Murcar golf course. Bud remembers that there was a strict hierarchy with golfers travelling at the front of the railcar and caddies in the rear compartment. An eventful ride was quite usual with the vehicle frequently coming off the rails especially by the 15th hole where there was a decided curve. The caddies were conscripted by Jim Fiddes and by means of levers kept on board and a bit of shouting and swearing the railcar would be righted. Re-railing the vehicle was not too difficult because of its lightweight build and the number of helping hands available.

Income from fares had been decreasing year by year and in January 1939 discussions were openly being held about the transit arrangements because of the continual deficit. It was suggested that the rail service be completely done away with in view of the many buses which now passed along the main road from the Bridge of Don. Timetables of the available bus services were posted at the clubhouse and members advised to be aware of them. Any more drastic steps with regard to the railway service were deferred meantime which was fortuitous in view of the transport problems to be endured later during the war.

In May 1939 the wheels of the Wickham railcar were so flat that the flanges were cutting into the bolts of the fishplates on the track. They were re-tyred by Cassie of King Street, Aberdeen but castings were also ordered from Wickham & Co. at a cost of £14 for replacement at a later date.

The Murcar Buggy at the wooden platform with driver Jim Fiddes.

courtesy Alan W. Brotchie

Chapter Twelve

The Second World War

On the outbreak of war in September 1939 petrol rationing was brought into force. The petrol tank sited at the clubhouse was half full at the time. Petrol had to be supplied in not less than 200-gallon deliveries. As the club could not take this quantity it was feared that it would be necessary to withdraw the rail service altogether. A notice to this effect was even put in the newspapers.

Fortunately, the implementation of the rationing scheme was delayed for a week, being introduced on 22nd September, 1939 during which time the tank had emptied sufficiently to allow the lub to receive a petrol delivery. A very restricted service was put in place consisting of one return trip only on Wednesday and two trips each way on Saturday and Sunday. An application was made to the Divisional Petroleum Officer in Dundee to authorise Murcar Golf Club to use petrol. The club was advised that any time they made an application for petrol coupons their request would be favourably considered.

In September 1939 Jim Fiddes approached the convenor reminding him that he had not had a half day off work since Smith the relief driver had left. It was decided that he be paid an additional five shillings for every week he worked without a day off. In November the timetable was revised, giving one return trip daily and two return trips at the weekend.

On Thursday 14th March, 1940 there was a repeat incident when tickets were stolen from the railcar while it was standing at the clubhouse. The police caught the boys responsible though not all the tickets were recovered. Under new regulations in 1940 the petrol pump had to be immobilized but arrangements were made to ensure continued supplies of petrol. A further 160 gallons were granted and an amended timetable with more journeys was approved to commence on Saturday 13th April, 1940.

The Wickham railcar had been out of service for nine months waiting on spare parts, gearing and pinions. Because of war requirements they had been delayed and were not delivered till April 1940. With the problems associated with the supply of fuel this was untimely since during this period the older railcar had to be used. The older vehicle's petrol consumption was almost double, giving only ten miles per gallon compared to 18 miles per gallon for the Wickham railcar.

Jim Rae remembers that as a young boy of five years old his family was visiting the area round about this time. He heard a train coming and was amazed to see what looked like a railway carriage running along, stop and start again. He had never seen such a thing and ran home to tell his father that he had seen a train with no steam engine pulling it! Jim couldn't get his father's nose out of his newspaper and turned to his mother who just smiled and said "Yes dear, that's nice".

Fiddes requested an increase in wages in April 1940. In view of the conditions at the time, the fact that he was also working on the course as well as driving, and the difficulty of finding another driver should he resign, it was agreed to grant him an additional ten shillings per week.

Under powers which could be exercised under the Defence Regulations 1939 Act, golf courses could be taken over for the training of troops. Murcar Golf Club continued operations but defensive features including barbed wire and mines were placed on the course. An air raid shelter for the steward and his family was also built at the clubhouse. Regulations in September 1940 stipulated that the club had

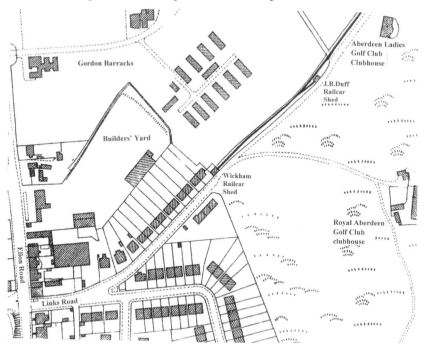

Bridge of Don in 1947 showing the new layout after the brickyard had closed and the second shed built to house the Wickham railcar.

map created by the author based on map by the Ordnance Survey,
reproduced with kind permission

to allow the Civil Defence contractors, Messrs Mowlem & Co. to use the club's petrol. By November 1940 the work was finished and the golf club renewed its applications for petrol coupons.

By March 1941 the petrol supply had become more dependable and the rail service was improved. This was particularly welcome in view of the increased numbers of people requiring transport. In April local boys broke 40 panes of glass in the older railcar and three panes in the car shed. The windows were boarded up as a result.

All members of the golf course staff were given an increase in wages in April 1941. The driver was given a war bonus of five shillings per week. An additional five shillings was granted as from May giving the driver a weekly wage of £4. In July 1941 an additional man, George Jolly, was engaged because Mr Munro the greenkeeper had been called up. He was to work on the course and also learn to drive the railcar as it was intended that he should take the place of Jim Fiddes who was taking Munro's place but also acting as relief driver on one Sunday each month. Jolly did not have an auspicious beginning though, driving into the shed and breaking the door. His wages were increased from £3 to £3 5s. in September 1941 and in April 1942 to £3 10s., but in consequence of this latest increase he now had to take on the duties on Sundays instead of Fiddes.

In July 1942 another new driver, James Fraser was appointed to take the place of Jolly who had left. He also had to work on the course and received a weekly wage of £3 5s. Fiddes was remunerated with £3 for the extra time he spent over a period of two weeks training the new driver. Fraser came off driving duties in August and Fiddes returned to being the usual driver and received an extra £1 10s. per week for longer hours being worked.

In September 1942 Kenneth MacKintosh, painter, was asked to provide an estimate for painting the railcar. He quoted £10 but it was decided to defer the matter for a while until such time as the whin bushes along the railway line could be cut back because the new paintwork would be scratched (it's not clear which railcar this was).

The condition of the railway at this time can be judged from the comments made by a visitor on behalf of *The Railway Observer* magazine of September 1942. He noted that "the railway was still in existence but not being used, the railcar being parked outside the golf house." This seems a strange observation and I think that the visit must have been a fleeting one and to a casual observer it might have appeared that the railway was disused because of the forlorn nature of the line at that particular time overgrown with whins and weeds. The stationary railcar in need of a good repaint would not have helped to give an impression of frequent usage. The whins were eventually cut back and the line was tidied up but it wasn't until April 1943 that it was finally agreed to have the car painted.

The railway needed to carry even more passengers than normal because members who would have otherwise travelled by private motor car could not do so. Petrol was rationed and after 1942 was totally banned for private motoring. Armed forces personnel were admitted as temporary members, as were golfers from Balnagask Golf Course who were granted temporary membership of Murcar Golf Club because they were prohibited from using their own course which was occupied by gun emplacements.

Aberdeen's worst air raid occurred on 21st April, 1943. One of the first targets was Gordon Barracks. The premises of Messrs John Joss & Sons were hit by German bombers and the spare Ford engine for the Wickham railcar which was stored there was destroyed. At a meeting in June 1943, it was agreed that the driver should be paid overtime for the extra hours worked at the rate of £2 per week during the summer months April to September and £1 per week during the winter months October to March. An indication of the long hours worked can be gauged from the fact that the last car was scheduled to depart from the clubhouse at 10.00 pm on Saturday nights. By August 1943 the threat of invasion had virtually gone. The club requested that tank traps be removed from the course but the reply was that it was not the policy to do so at present, the chief reason being shortage of labour. In November 1943 some carpentry repairs were done to the railcar free of charge by club member George Dow.

Due to some misunderstanding it was not realised until December 1944 that the spare engine had been destroyed in the air raid of the previous year. Despite the fact that the period had elapsed during which claims could be lodged, the club made a claim for £26 10s. and it was paid in full by the insurance company in February 1945.

The end of the war in 1945 was celebrated with the Victory Day Holiday on Saturday, 8th June, 1946. A special more frequent railcar service was arranged for that day. The contribution made by the railway to the survival of Murcar Golf Club was recognised by the chairman who stated in the annual report: *"The Club was indeed fortunate in getting sufficient petrol to maintain a restricted service during the war years, and had it been otherwise it is doubtful if the Club could have carried on."*

Chapter Thirteen

The Final Years

In May 1946 the terms and conditions of employment for the driver were clarified. Previously, special payments had been made for extra duties based on a gentleman's agreement. It was felt that this was unsatisfactory and henceforth he was to receive a firm wage with no extras. This was to be £5 per week for a six-day week, with one day each week being allowed free. The driver was to refrain from touching alcohol while on duty with the car. On Wednesday and Saturday mornings the driver would work solely on the maintenance of the railcar and railway line. Jim Fiddes agreed to the conditions but at the same time asked whether he could be employed purely as a greenkeeper, but that wasn't possible at the time.

The railcars had not had a major overhaul for many years and the permanent way now required maintenance and repair. An inspection was conducted in November 1946 and it was reported that the track was badly overgrown with whins in several places so Fiddes and the green staff set about the clearance.

In February 1947 Fiddes was granted an increase of another five shillings in wages. The engine for the Wickham railcar needed replacing so in August 1947 the old second-hand engine was inspected by Messrs Claud Hamilton who were authorised to overhaul it for £37.

In October 1947 the safety implications of the railcar carrying heavy loads became a concern. Members of the transit committee decided that they and Fiddes should inspect the railway and discuss possible improvements. Restrictions on the number of passengers carried had been imposed at various times in the past, figures of 36, 35 and 32 all being stipulated as the maximum number permissible. These conditions had been imposed both by insurance policies and by Murcar Golf Club in order to reduce wear and tear on the railcar.

Since the railway was the only means of transport for many people it was preferable to take the extra passengers onboard rather than making an additional run to return for them which would have caused delay and used more petrol. Anecdotes about the overcrowding are of course now recalled with affection. It was often just a case of everybody just piling on. On one memorable journey, the older railcar carried 76 passengers; sitting inside, standing around the edge, perched on the roof radiator, and draped over the roof.

Other forms of ill-advised behaviour were not unknown. The Royal Aberdeen Golf Club had occasion to complain about Murcar golfers throwing articles at Royal Aberdeen golfers in an attempt to put them off their stroke as the railcar passed. Especially at weekends, residents of Links Road were often upset by the rowdy behaviour of golfers walking past after catching the last trip home.

Petrol rationing was still in force, but a more frequent timetable was possible because of an increase in the club's petrol allocation. In October 1947 for example the convenor reported that he still had an ample supply and did not need to apply for extra coupons. Approximately eight gallons of petrol were being used every week. Then the Ministry of Fuel and Power decided to withdraw the petrol entitlement altogether. After considerable negotiations the Ministry agreed to continue, but the ration was not as much as the club wished. Despite much correspondence and repeated applications right into 1948 the Ministry refused to grant an increased quota of petrol. Relationships with the petrol issuing authorities had actually been more cordial during the war.

Jim Fiddes starting up the engine of the Murcar Buggy with the cranking handle in 1948.
courtesy Aberdeen Bon-Accord and Northern Pictorial

Jim Fiddes made a request that he be taken off driving duties in February but by April he was not so sure so the matter was held in abeyance. In August, when the Wickham railcar was under repair again it was agreed that there would always be trouble until the trackwork was attended to. A railway linesman to execute the necessary work was sought.

In September 1948 an inspection of the railway line was made by the secretary and the transit committee convenor accompanied by Mr A.

Finnie who was an inspector of linesmen with British Railways. It transpired that the general condition of the line was not too bad, but it was felt that the first stage should be a complete clearance of all undergrowth and bushes from the permanent way. W. J. Anderson Ltd submitted an estimate of £500 to do the work but it was decided not to pursue the matter for the time being. The committee considered purchasing an ex-army flame thrower at a cost of £10 10s. which would be effective in clearing whins and undergrowth.

The railway was still handy for conveying golfers during competitions but just piling onto the vehicle could lead to accidents. During the Northern Open held on Friday 29th April, 1949 Walter Lyle, a well-known Scottish professional had to withdraw from the competition when he fell from the car on his way to the course and sustained a shoulder injury.

Various amendments were now being made to the timetable because certain runs of the railcar were not being utilised by the members. E.N.C. Haywood recalled the scene at that time whilst out for a walk one afternoon: *"One day I discovered the Bridge of Don terminus quite by chance, and luckily happened to be there just as the Wickham car turned up. This left*

Murcar Buggy travelling south past the eleventh tee of the Royal Aberdeen Golf Course at Balgownie. The golfer is actually a Murcar member, the vehicle having stopped at a suitable location for a posed photograph taken in 1948. When real Royal Aberdeen Golf Club golfers were playing at this location, they sometimes had occasion to complain because Murcar members passing in the buggy would try to put them off their stroke.

courtesy Aberdeen Bon-Accord and Northern Pictorial

again without any wait, departing as empty as when it arrived." Some income could be derived from non-golfers. Stuart Milne remembers his family going for a walk along the beach in the final year of operation. His father treated them to a ride on the older railcar.

Between February and September 1949 Messrs Stainer & Cairns, builders, 25 Ellon Road, did repair work on parts of the railway line which were in bad condition. In August though, it was agreed that no unnecessary extra expenses including overtime should be incurred. At the October 1949 annual general meeting it was stated that a large amount of work had been carried out both to the line and the railcars and was essential because the service had to be maintained for the convenience of members. The problem was that the deficit had increased every year and fewer members were using the service. With

The Wickham railcar as depicted in the local press when the service ended in June 1950. There is a deal of artistic licence, since the background street scene does not really reflect the route of the railway. It certainly does show the buggy in its fondly remembered state of being overcrowded and bouncing over the track. Jim Fiddes, the last and longest serving driver is ringing the bell. *courtesy Evening Express*

the advent of better roads and ownership of private cars increasing, there was less of a requirement for the rail service and the club felt the need to economise. Mr Bryson submitted a scheme being considered for taxis to be run from the Bridge of Don to the clubhouse. This would allow the railcars to be retired thereby saving running expenses and allowing Jim Fiddes to be available for full-time work on the course. By January 1950 the arrangements had been finalised with W.G. Pirie, General Merchant and Motor Hirer, 801 King Street, Aberdeen. These premises were at the south side of the bridge beside the Aberdeen tram terminus. It was agreed that the Murcar Golf Club railcar should finally be withdrawn from service on 31st January, 1950 and that from 1st February, 1950 the taxi service would replace it.

The arrangements were as follows:

1. The timetable would be published from time to time and the taxis would run from the Bridge of Don to the clubhouse.
2. The firm would charge the club 4s. 6d. per run.
3. Members would be charged sixpence per run each way.
4. Tickets for the run would be obtained on arrival at the clubhouse and at the clubhouse prior to departure.
5. Jim Fiddes was now to work full-time on the golf course at a reduced wage of £5 per week.

After the first week's service some alterations were made. Tickets were now to be issued and paid for at the Bridge of Don. Mr Pirie, the proprietor was also instructed to phone the clubhouse before proceeding on his journey at night in order to ensure that there were members waiting to be conveyed back to town and so save unnecessary journeys. When petrol rationing was finally lifted in May 1950 it meant even fewer members would use the rail service because they had the use of their private motor cars again. To help the club's finances it was suggested that passengers getting a lift home from friends might care to donate sixpence to the transit fund.

At the beginning of June 1950, it was learned that Mr W.G. Pirie was disposing of his taxis on 15th June and the service would no longer be available. While it was felt that the rail service was expensive there was no alternative, so the railcar was reprieved for a fortnight and put into operation again. The last scheduled rail service was made by the Wickham railcar on Friday 30th June, 1950. Hilton Taxis of Anderson Avenue, Woodside, Aberdeen was offered the contract and took over the

A 1950s view of the clubhouse of Murcar Golf Club. The body of the Wickham railcar is on the right.   *courtesy Murcar Links Golf Club*

service on 1st July, 1950. The outlay for the club was still considerable and voluntary contributions were encouraged by means of a subscription box placed in the clubhouse.

In October 1950 it was found that the old wooden car shed had become insecure particularly because of recent heavy winds. If the older railcar could be sold for scrap, then the shed could be dismantled by the green staff and the wood utilised elsewhere. An offer of £5 for scrap was made in November by J.R. Ross & Son, 31 Princes Street, Aberdeen but was refused. The older railcar was driven to the clubhouse end of the railway line and parked there until such time as its fate was decided and the shed was dismantled. The first plan for the retired railcar was to do some modifications and then make it into a shelter. This didn't happen though and by February 1951 it was decided to make it available to the club steward for use as a bottle and general store.

The transit committee convenor had by February 1951 arranged a flat fare charge for the taxis. It was to be £12 each for each of the six winter months and £30 for the summer months. By June 1951 arrangements with the taxi company were unsatisfactory so a new contract from 1st July, 1951 was made with Clifton Taxis, 402 Clifton Road, Aberdeen.

The Wickham railcar had been kept for emergencies but by August 1951 it was generally agreed that it was most unlikely that it would ever be used again. The corrugated-iron car shed and rails were advertised for sale, the offer to include cost of removal. The shed was then sold to the 46th Troop of Boy Scouts for £100.

An offer from Motherwell Machinery and Scrap Company of £1850 for the trackwork was accepted. The firm wished to have the use of the Wickham railcar stripped of its coachwork for transporting the rails and sleepers to the Bridge of Don and that thereafter the chassis and engine would be available for the club. On one occasion the scrap company's driver was a bit too enthusiastic and there was some unplanned demolition work when he crashed into the door to the shed which was now the Boy Scouts' hut.

The trackwork in its final days was in extremely poor condition with the webs of some rails rusted right through. It was lifted between October and December 1951, taking a bit longer than expected because of adverse weather conditions. After the New Year when the job was complete it was noticed that the scrap company had removed the chassis and engine. Murcar Golf Club wrote asking that they return the old engine as previously arranged because it could be kept as a spare for the golf course tractor.

During the winter months of 1951 the taxi service had been curtailed because so few passengers were using it. Murcar Golf Club still had to pay the charges regardless. Throughout the summer of 1952 it was obvious that the taxi service was getting insufficient support from members and it was becoming a greater expense for the club. Clifton Taxis had also intimated in June that the contract price would have to be increased in view of recent increases in the price of petrol. The number of journeys was adjusted in order that the contract price would remain the same.

There were buses, running from Mealmarket Street in Aberdeen which passed the top of the road to the course and although the outward service was adequate, the service back into town was infrequent. So it was agreed that for the time being the taxi service should continue. Then in August 1952 it was decided that there was no need for a taxi service going out to the course but they would still be provided to return to Aberdeen.

Murcar Golf Club wanted to abolish the taxi service, but Mr Ewan, a new club member and the proprietor of a taxi firm, had expressed his willingness to cooperate in operating a modified service. In September 1952 a service for the winter timetable was arranged. The fare was increased to ninepence for a single run and a shilling for a double run. Later, because of complications with the tickets, the fare was standardised at ninepence for each journey. By the middle of November 1952, the receipts amounted to only 12s. 6d. and the club was faced with a bill of £9. It was therefore decided to discontinue the taxi service completely. All forms of transport provided by Murcar Golf Club then ceased.

A group of golfers pose in front of the Murcar Buggy in the 1930s. This view provides a good illustration of the state of the track.   *courtesy Murcar Links Golf Club*

Chapter Fourteen

Subsequent History and Remains

In 1953 the older railcar was allocated for the storage of caddy cars belonging to members of the ladies' section. The body of the Wickham railcar was in use as the main caddy car store for gentlemen members. It was also decided to dispose of the Wickham railcar's Ford engine as scrap. The Wickham railcar body was still in use as a caddy cart shed at Murcar Golf Club in the 1960s.

In 1959 the sunken trackbed at the terminus on Links Road was filled in and the platform face was removed. In 1960 part of the platform at the clubhouse survived and railway sleepers were still in place at some locations.

The railway had always constituted the western boundary of Royal Aberdeen Golf Club. In 1964 the Royal Aberdeen bought Links of Balgownie Farm buildings and land with a view to making improvements in the future. Much of the increased acreage was to the west of the railway. Murcar Golf Club which enjoyed a good relationship with the Royal Aberdeen Golf Club gifted the trackbed of the old railway for a nominal sum so as not to impose any restrictions on any expansion plans. On Links Road the corrugated-iron car shed for the Wickham buggy was demolished in 1999 to make room for an imposing new entrance to The Royal Aberdeen Golf Club.

A photograph of the Wickham railcar in 1960 when it was in use as a caddy cart store. This view shows the front and left-hand side.

photograph by Norris Forrest,
courtesy of Great North of Scotland Railway Association

At Blackdog the westernmost part of the brickworks site was fenced off in 2001 and a building belonging to Donside Safety Supplies erected. Most of the brickworks site however has not been built over and is covered with brick rubble. Red brick paving is still in place just under the earth. The positions of the machinery building and the larger Hoffmann kiln can still be seen among the vegetation, their unique shapes visible on a Google Earth satellite image.

The former clay pits were still visible as such until 2003 when the ground was levelled off. The area between the buildings sloping down to the clay pits was also levelled and cleared in 2005.

The original railway terminus and brickyard of the Seaton Brick and Tile Company Limited was the site of John Joss, Sand and Gravel Merchants, until 2003 when the Joss Court flats were built by Barratt Homes.

At the annual general meeting of Murcar Golf Club in November 2005 it was unanimously agreed that the word "Links" should be reinstated in the club's name so now the title is Murcar Links Golf Club. The eleventh hole at the club is still known as "Railway".

It is still possible to follow the route of the railway for a great deal of its length. From the entrance of The Royal Aberdeen Golf Club the route of the railway is between the iron railings and the pathway past the clubhouse of the Aberdeen Ladies Golf Club. Hidden behind the trees Burnside Farm buildings still exist after being taken over by for use by the army.

Just south of Links of Balgownie Farm there is a section of line where the indentations made by the railway sleepers show in a good light. On both golf courses the old railway cuttings in particular are discernible as whin bushes have grown in them. This is especially the case along the boundary with the farmland where the line can easily be followed. North of Murcar Links Golf Club clubhouse the geographical features have altered considerably. Strabathie Hill is not the prominent feature it once was because of excavations which have taken place over the years.

The culverts built to carry the railway over the Burn of Mundurno, Tarbot Burn and Blackdog Burn remain in place, as does the railway embankment over the Blackdog Burn. During the last hundred years the burn has changed its course and the dunes have increased in extent and height. Between the embankment and the site of the brickworks the fields have been levelled off and trees have been planted.

The three-storey block called Seaton Cottages erected for the employees and the single cottage for the works foreman are still there. The block has been renamed Strabathie Cottages and the foreman's house has been named Seaton Cottage. The Seaton Brick and Tile Company Limited head office building in 180/180 South Market Street, Aberdeen is now occupied by N.B. Surveys.

The hand-bell which was rung to announce the departure of the buggy is in the trophy display cabinet of Murcar Links Golf Club. A maker's plate from the Wickham railcar is in the care of Aberdeen Transport Society. A travel ticket for the Murcar Buggy is held in the Wingate H. Bett ticket collection in Birmingham Central Library. The author also has an original ticket.

There are examples of Seaton Brick and Tile Company Limited bricks held in the collection of Aberdeen City Council Art Gallery and Museums. Mark Cranston has examples preserved in his large collection of Scottish bricks. The author has several bricks of different styles produced by the company. An original 1899 wooden sleeper complete with metal spikes has been preserved by the author and still smells strongly of creosote.

This photograph was taken in 1960 and shows the railway embankment and culvert over the Burn of Mundurno. In the foreground there is a sluicegate and a wooden footbridge. In the background "Strabathie Castle" is on the summit of the Hill of Strabathie.

photograph by Norris Forrest,
courtesy of Great North of Scotland Railway Association

Appendix One

Strabathie Brickworks Song

Dan Fraser was a popular Scotch vocal comedian who played in music halls and theatres in England and Northern Ireland as well as all over Scotland. Once employed by the company and worked at Strabathie, he entertained the guests at the 1905 annual concert and dance of The Seaton Brick and Tile Benevolent Society. His performance included a song specially composed by him. The words were written in "Doric", the dialect of the north-east of Scotland. Quoiting is prominent, the pastime which was popular with all brick-workers in Britain. He reminded the audience that the condition of the track and rolling stock was not exactly suitable for high-speed running. It certainly appears from the flavour of the song that the workers were not unhappy in their work and that relations with the management were cordial.

Hurrah for the Boys that work among the Clay

Noo, of a' the jobs that I wis at, there's ane I liked just gran'; **ane: one**
'Twas workin' at "Strabathie",'mang the clay, ye'll understan'.
Some days I fed the pipe machine, sometimes I cairried coal,
An' ma muscles fairly got a rax doon in the big clay hole. **rax: strain**

Patter and Chorus –
    Hurrah for the boys that work among the clay,
    They are as happy as a king in his high station;
    At fitba' they can kick as weel as mak' a brick,
    And at quoiting, man, they'd fairly lick creation.

Noo, the first day that I worked there, I was an awfu' sicht; **sicht: sight**
I wis covered wi' clay heid tae feet ere I got hame at nicht;
Ma wife she looks me up an' doon, says she then, wi' a sneer –
"If yer workin' noo among the clay, well, dinna bring it here."

Patter and Chorus –

Auld Peter, wi' his engine, fairly trails ye ower the line, **rummel: jolt**
An' the way ye rummel in yer seats, it's like preens gaun up yer spine; **preens: pins**
But ye jist maun grin an' bear it, it's very hard, nae doot; **maun: must**
Ye ken if he gaed faster, chaps, ye a' micht tummle oot.

Patter and Chorus –

The gaffers are a genial lot, they are, upon my soul,
An' noo an' then, frae oot the kilns, "Bully"* gie's a howl.
The pipe squad an' the brick squad, aye, an; the ither men,
Better pals ye canna get, so we'll roar oot since again –

Patter and Chorus –

* Mr Bull (it is common to add a diminutive suffix of "ie" or "y" to names)

Costs of building the Strabathie Light Railway

Notes and prior estimates of costs etc.
James Watt, Supervisor
Messrs. Walker & Duncan, Civil Engineers, 3 Golden Square, Aberdeen

DETAILS	COST
7000 sleepers @ 1s. 10½d.	£656
206 tons of 41¼ lbs/in rail @ £5 19s.	£1,226
7 tons of fishplates, bolts etc @ £10	£70
Points & crossings	£80
Earthworks 11,000 cubic yards	£458
Ballasting	£143
Platelaying	£143
Carting rails etc	£50
Load at depot	£40
Engine shed	£150
Culverts	£120
Dams	£50
Fencing	£150
The Writing is Indecipherable	£26
The Writing is Indecipherable	£30
23 wagons @ £30	£690
Engine	£684
TOTAL about	£5,000

This view shows that there was a footboard only on one side of the vehicle. Passenger access to the compartment was via sliding doors which were also on the same side. This was the side of the vehicle which always faced east, facing the roadway at the terminus and the platform at the clubhouse.

courtesy Aberdeen Bon-Accord and Northern Pictorial

DATE	ACCOUNT
Mar 31 1899	Charles Cowie, Cartwright & General Blacksmith, 184 West North Street, Aberdeen
"	John Fleming & Co., Wood Merchants, Albert Sawmills, Albert Quay, Aberdeen
May 31 1899	Alexander Christie's Outlays
June 30 1899	Advocate's Society for same
"	Wages
June 31 1899	J. Davidson
"	John Yeoman, Cartwright, 604 King Street, Aberdeen
"	J. Beatson & Son
"	Alexander Hutcheon, Joiner, Murcar
"	John Yeoman, Cartwright, 604 King Street, Aberdeen
"	Scottish Employers Liability Assurance Co., 9 King Street, Aberdeen
"	George Cassie, General Blacksmith, 600 King Street, Aberdeen
"	C & P.H. Chalmers, 18 Golden Square, Aberdeen
"	Caledonian Railway Company
"	Wages
Aug 31 1899	William Fraser, Carter, Dunbar Street, Aberdeen
"	Robert Fraser, Farmer & Carter, Brickfield Place, Aberdeen
"	d. Gray & Son, Wheelwrights & Blacksmiths, 180 to 190 Hardgate, Aberdeen
"	Edward Sisterson
"	Mutter Howe & Co., Carrier
"	William Topp, Contractor
"	Wages
Sep 30 1899	City Parish Council
"	Aberdeen, Newcastle & Hull Steam Co. Ltd
"	Captain Paterson
"	Charles Calder & Co., Timber Merchants, 15 Baltic Chambers, Newcastle
"	Wordie & Co., Railway Agents & Carriers, 16 Schoolhill, Aberdeen
"	W.R. Aiken, Ship & Insurance Broker, 53 Regent Quay, Aberdeen
"	Insurance on Sleepers
"	Alexander Hutcheon, Joiner, Murcar
"	d. Maxwell, Junior
"	Wages
"	Credit by Cash Account
Oct 31 1899	Edward Sisterson
"	Alexander Hutcheon, Joiner, Murcar
"	John Hart
"	Harbour Commissioners
"	John Fleming & Co., Wood Merchants, Albert Sawmills, Albert Quay, Aberdeen
"	Mearns, Slessor & Smith's expenses
"	Wages
Nov 30 1899	Wordie & Co., Railway Agents & Carriers, 16 Schoolhill, Aberdeen
"	Edward Sisterson
"	C & P.H. Chalmers, 18 Golden Square, Aberdeen
"	Douglas Duncan, Advocates, 23 Crown Street, Aberdeen
"	Lachlan MacKinnon & Son, Advocates, 23 Market Street, Aberdeen
"	John Nicol, Tenant of Findlay Farm
"	Harbour Dues & Weighing
"	Wordie & Co., Railway Agents & Carriers, 16 Schoolhill, Aberdeen
"	Alexander Hutcheon, Joiner, Murcar
"	W.R. Aiken, Ship & Insurance Broker, 53 Regent Quay, Aberdeen

DETAILS	COST		
	£7	14s.	-
	£4	17s.	10d.
	£3	10s.	-
	£1	5s.	-
Wages	£193	18s.	-
	-	4s.	6d.
	£3	12s.	-
	£32	1s.	4d.
Fencing	£8	6s.	10d.
	£1	4s.	10d.
Insurance	£2	8s.	9d.
	£1	17s.	2d.
	£2	2s.	2d.
	£7	3s.	6d.
Wages	£291	3s.	1d.
Cartage	£2	11s.	6d.
Cartage	£1	15s.	-
	£7	10s.	-
Rails	£11	6s.	9d.
Cartage	-	12s.	6d.
	£1	4s.	9d.
Wages	£154	18s.	1d.
	-	8s.	9d.
	-	1s.	5d.
Freight on Sleepers	£51	1s.	-
Wooden Sleepers	£582	10s.	3d.
Cartage	£1	14s.	-
Labourage	£5	16s.	3d.
Insurance on Sleepers	-	19s.	6d.
Fencing	£100	-	-
	-	17s.	-
Wages	£74	13s.	4d.
Credit	£5	10s.	3d.
Rails	£922	19s.	3d.
Fencing	£70	-	-
	£6	6s.	7d.
	£10	5s.	8d.
	£1	19s.	6d.
Director's expenses	£15	-	-
Wages	£84	8s.	11d.
Cartage	£23	12s.	10d.
Rails	£682	2s.	11d.
Rent	£2	14s.	-
Rent	£1	10s.	9d.
Rent	£2	19s.	3d.
Rent for Ballast Pit	£5	-	-
Harbour Dues & Weighing	£3	18s.	5d.
Cartage	£10	1s.	1d.
Fencing	£51	7s.	6d.
Labourage	£66	14s.	5d.

DATE	ACCOUNT
Dec 31 1899	Edward Sisterson
"	Charles Calder & Co., Timber Merchants, 15 Baltic Chambers, Newcastle
"	John Miller & Co., Sandilands Chemical Works, Miller Street, Aberdeen
"	Davidson & Garden, Advocates
"	Duncan Forbes Trustees
"	George Cassie, General Blacksmith, 600 King Street, Aberdeen
"	Hudswell Clarke & Co. Leeds, Locomotive Works
"	W.G. Bagnall Ltd, Stafford, Locomotive Works
"	Wages
Jan 31 1900	Wordie & Co., Railway Agents & Carriers, 16 Schoolhill, Aberdeen
"	John Yeoman, Cartwright, 604 King Street, Aberdeen
"	John McAdam & Sons, Carriers & Contractors, 47,49 Charlotte Street, Aberdeen
"	Alexander Hutcheon, Joiner, Murcar
"	Wordie & Co., Railway Agents & Carriers, 16 Schoolhill, Aberdeen
"	Wages
Feb 28 1900	William Walker & Son, Ironmongers, 28 Netherkirkgate, Aberdeen
"	Wordie & Co., Railway Agents & Carriers, 16 Schoolhill, Aberdeen
"	Wages
Mar 31 1900	P. Buyers, Chandlers, Regent Quay, Aberdeen
"	James Leith, Contractor
"	Wages
Apl 30 1900	Hudswell Clarke & Co. Leeds, Locomotive Works
"	Dick Kerr & Co. Engineering, Kilmarnock
"	Wages
"	Torry Horse Account (expenses)
"	Sales Ledger Account
"	Depot Wages Account
"	Account Payable Account
"	Credit by Rolling Stock Account
May 31 1900	Alexander Hutcheon, Joiner, Murcar
"	Lachlan MacKinnon & Son, Advocates, 23 Market Street, Aberdeen
"	Wages
Jun 30 1900	Aberdeen Town Council
"	W.G. Bagnall Ltd, Stafford, Locomotive Works
"	Alexander Hutcheon, Joiner, Murcar
"	Wages
Jul 31 1900	George Cassie, General Blacksmith, 600 King Street, Aberdeen
"	Wages
Sep 30 1900	William McKinnon & Co. Engineers, 20 Spring Garden, Aberdeen
Nov 30 1900	William Topp, Contractor
"	Alexander Hutcheon, Joiner, Murcar
Dec 31 1900	Aberdeen, Newcastle & Hull Steam Co. Ltd
"	George Cassie, General Blacksmith, 600 King Street, Aberdeen
"	Thom & Strachan, Plumbers, Gasfitters, 62 Windmill Brae & 474 Union St., Aber
Jan 31 1900	William McKinnon & Co. Engineers, 20 Spring Garden, Aberdeen
"	Edward Sisterson
Mar 31 1900	Messrs. Walker & Duncan, Civil Engineers, 3 Golden Square, Aberdeen
Apl 30 1900	Credit by Rolling Stock Account

DETAILS	COST		
Rails	£10	-	-
Wooden Sleepers	£33	2s.	2d.
	-	8s.	-
Rent to Seaton Estate	£6	4s.	6d.
Rent	£16	3s.	6d.
	£38	1s.	8d.
Steam Locomotive	£875	-	-
Goods Wagons	£335	-	-
Wages	£92	2s.	3d.
Cartage	£1	1s.	-
	£5	12s.	10d.
Cartage	£1	5s.	-
Fencing	£46	10s.	11d.
Cartage	£5	-	-
Wages	£84	6s.	11d.
	-	12s.	6d.
Cartage	£1	5s.	9d.
Wages	£33	9s.	11d.
	-	17s.	-
	£1	12s.	-
Wages	£52	9s.	5d.
Steam Locomotive Costs	£3	3s.	9d.
Purchase of Pointwork	£40	-	-
Wages	£2	5s.	10d.
Expenses	£205	-	-
	£203	11s.	8d.
Prop. Manager Salary	£80	-	-
	-	18s.	8d.
Credit	£1,213	3s.	9d.
Fencing	£43	3s.	8d.
Rent	£4	-	-
Wages	£15	16s.	9d.
Purchase four Tramcars	£65	-	-
Wheelsets for Trams	£50	-	-
Fencing	£20	12s.	3d.
Wages	£48	18s.	8d.
	£32	18s.	8d.
Wages	£111	9s.	11d.
Constructing Pointwork	£22	13s.	6d.
	£10	3s.	3d.
Fencing	£20	15s.	2d.
	-	2s.	4d.
	£6	9s.	8d.
	£19	14s.	10d.
Constructing Pointwork	£14	19s.	6d.
Rails	£36	7s.	10d.
Civil Engineers Costs	£213	4s.	11d.
Credit	£122	-	-
TOTAL	£5,112	10s.	5d.

Appendix Three

Permanent Way

It was originally estimated by James Watt the supervisor of Messrs Walker & Duncan, Civil Engineers, 3 Golden Square, Aberdeen that 206 tons of rail and seven tons of fishplates, bolts etc would be required for the construction of the railway.

The rails were 30 ft lengths of lightweight flat bottom 41¼ lbs per yard and were supplied by Edward Sisterson, Iron Merchant, 26 Side, Woodley Field, Hexham, Northumberland for a total cost of £1662 16s. 9d.

The points and crossings were supplied by Dick, Kerr & Co. Ltd, Britannia Engineering Works, Kilmarnock in January 1900 for £40. The pointwork had originally been intended for a South American railway but had been delayed for financial reasons. The construction of the pointwork was then undertaken by William McKinnon & Co. Engineers, 20 Spring Garden, Aberdeen at a cost of £37 13s.

The sleepers laid in 1899 and 1900 were a quantity of about 7000 creosoted Baltic redwood measuring 8 in. x 4 in. x 6 ft long supplied by Charles Calder & Company, Timber Merchants, 15 Baltic Chambers, Newcastle-upon-Tyne for £616 0s. 5d. They were shipped to Aberdeen by, the Aberdeen, Newcastle and Hull Steam Company, Limited.

A detailed description of the trackwork when built was as follows:

The gauge is 3 feet; the weight of the rails is 41¼ lbs. per yard, with fishplates 14 ½ inches long, weighing 13 lbs per pair, and laid on creosoted Baltic redwood sleepers 8 inches by 4 inches by 6 feet long. The rails are 30 feet long, and there are 11 sleepers to each rail, placed at 2 feet centres at rail joints, and the intermediate sleepers being at 2 feet 9½ inches centres, each 30 feet rail is secured to the sleepers as follows:- 2¾ inches fang bolts through each end of sleeper at rail joint with clip washers to catch rail flange (³⁄₁₆ in. clearance being left for expansion), ¾ inch diameter fang bolts through rail metal flange and centre sleeper, the other sleepers having dog spikes (⅝ inch square metal, 5¼ inches long) for securing rails. The rails were given an inward cant of about 1 in 20 by cutting a groove in the sleeper ⅛ inch deep at outside edge, and ¼ inch deep on inside edge.

Stone ballast was obtained from the nearby Findlay Farm when the railway was built. The Seaton Brick and Tile Company Limited then paid rent to Mr John Nicol, the tenant for use of a ballast pit on the farm.

Alexander Hutcheon, Carpenter, Cartwright and General Merchant of Cloverhill, Murcar got the contract for erecting 4000 yards of post and wire fencing. Six-feet long larch posts were used standing four-feet high after being driven two feet into the ground. Galvanised wire was stapled to the wood in either four or six lines depending on the location. This cost a total of £360 16s. 4d.

In May 1914 an advert was placed in the *Scotsman* newspaper addressed to wood merchants to quote for the supply of 1000 new redwood creosoted railway sleepers 6 feet by 8 inches by 4 inches, price to include delivery.

On 4th February, and 6th February, 1918 the Seaton Brick & Tile Co. Ltd. advertised considerable quantities of scrap metal, brass and old rails for sale in the Bridge of Don yard. Soon thereafter Aberdeen Scrap Metal Day was held on Saturday 16th February, 1918 at the request of the Ministry of Munitions. Whether sold or donated it is not clear why railway track was surplus to the requirements of the company.

After Murcar Golf Club purchased the railway in 1924 they did not need to purchase any new rails since they had inherited some extras. This included 70 lengths of rail obtained free of charge. Further repairs over the years were done by the local blacksmith, Mr Copland. One hundred steel rods were ordered at 2s. 7d. each in November 1925 and these were used at various locations to bind the rails together and maintain the gauge. In March 1929 80 to 90 old rails were sold off.

Over the years rotting wooden sleepers were reversed to spread out the wear. If this could not be done, they were sold and replaced by new ones of different sizes from various sources. In 1930 Murcar Golf Club purchased a large number of second-hand sleepers from the London Midland Scottish Railway for one shilling each. These were usually made of pinewood, these were 9 ft long and were cut in half for use, resulting in sleepers measuring 10 in. x 5 in. x 4 ft 6 in. long.

Three hundred wooden sleepers were bought in May 1933 and in 1936 100 new sleepers were bought for £11 13s. In 1936 Murcar Golf Club used gravel as ballast. In 1938 the golf club obtained a supply of 50 new creosoted sleepers measuring 7½ in. x 3½ in. x 4 ft-10 in. long from Alex McKenzie & Sons, Wood Merchants, 21 Willowdale Place, Aberdeen at three shillings each.

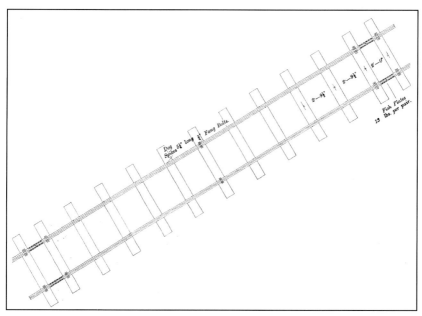

The original trackwork used 30 feet lengths of lightweight flat-bottom rail and creosoted Baltic redwood sleepers. The rails were bolted to the sleepers at the ends and in the middle, the other sleepers having spikes to secure the rails.

Aberdeen Association of Civil Engineers

Appendix Four

The Steam Locomotive

When construction of the railway started in June 1899 it was stated that W. G. Bagnall Ltd of Stafford was supplying the motive power. The locomotive depicted in the local press was a genuine W.G. Bagnall design of 1897 which could suggest that a tender had been submitted from that company.

A locomotive was instead ordered on 3rd July, 1899 from Hudswell Clarke & Company of Leeds at a cost of £875. The locomotive supplied was a four-wheeled saddle tank, a basic three-feet gauge contractor's steam locomotive. This particular design was such that design alterations could be made according to the customer's requirements. It was supplied painted in Midland Red livery, one of Hudswell Clarke's standard colours and was named *NEWBURGH*.

Manufacturer	Hudswell Clarke & Company, Leeds
Works Number:	545
Ordered:	3rd July, 1899
Promised Delivery:	November 1899
Ex Works date:	29th November 1899
Saddle Tank Locomotive	
Width:	7 ft 4 in.
Four-coupled (0-4-0ST)	
Outside Cylinders	
Diameter of Cylinders:	9 in.
Length of Stroke:	15 in.
Diameter of Wheels:	2 ft 3 in.
Wheelbase:	5 ft
Fuel Space:	17 cubic feet
Capacity of Tank:	300 gallons
Weight, in working order:	10tons, 13cwt, 1quarter (according to builder)
Weight, empty:	10½ tons
Weight, loaded:	12½ tons
Named:	*NEWBURGH*
Cost:	£875
Livery:	Hudswell Clarke Standard Midland Red
Gauge:	3 ft, axles arranged to suit 4 ft 8½ in. gauge

Two water gauge cocks

Central combined buffer and draw-gear "Chopper" type coupling set on the centre line 2 ft from rail level.

Steam locomotive manufactured by W.G. Bagnall as originally depicted for use on the railway.   *Bon Accord*

Below: A standard Hudswell Clarke 3 ft gauge 0-4-0 saddle tank contractors locomotive built in 1899. Small design alterations could be made according to the customer's requirements. This was the type supplied for the Strabathie Light Railway.

courtesy Ronald Nelson Redman

Hudswell Clarke steam locomotive *NEWBURGH* with crew and workers in 1903.

Aberdeen Daily Journal

Goods Wagons

It was originally thought that about 25 goods wagons would be needed for the railway to start operations. James Watt of Walker & Duncan, Civil Engineers, 3 Golden Square, Aberdeen was more exact; his estimated costs stated 23 wagons at £30 each.

The Seaton Brick and Tile Company Limited hoped to be given running powers over the Aberdeen Corporation Tramways lines along King Street. Alexander Christie designed dual gauge wagons with a capacity of four tons. One version had 4 ft 8½ in. standard gauge rail wheels fitted onto the axles of the 3 ft gauge wagons and another type had road wheels fitted onto the outside of the axles of the 3 ft gauge wagons. This would have allowed wagons to run straight off the Strabathie Railway tracks onto the tramlines or onto the road. Illustrations of these designs appeared in the local press in June 1899. Christie submitted the design to the Patent Office in 1899 but there are no records of the application being granted.

While the railway was under construction in July 1899 spoil was being carried along sections of track by wagons. It was stated that *"The waggons are so made that they could run over the Aberdeen tramway system…"*. Maybe the extent of their dual gauge capability at that time was just having extended axles which could accept another set of wheels. The author has no technical details about these wagons or who manufactured them.

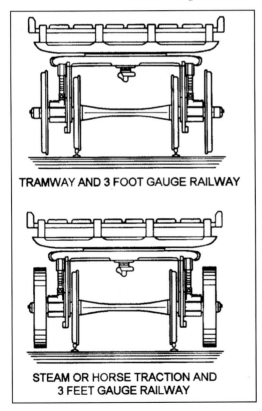

TRAMWAY AND 3 FOOT GAUGE RAILWAY

STEAM OR HORSE TRACTION AND 3 FEET GAUGE RAILWAY

Proposed dual gauge for running from the 3 ft gauge Strabathie Light Railway onto the road or on to the 4 ft 8½ in. tracks of Aberdeen Corporation Tramways.
Aberdeen Journal

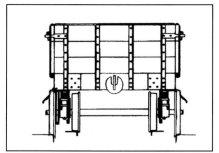

W.G. Bagnall three-plank dropside brick wagon. This is based on W.G. Bagnall drawings with narrow gauge and standard gauge wheels on the same axle.
Original drawing by A. Gordon Pirie based on W.G. Bagnall works drawing

Below: W.G. Bagnall three-plank dropside brick wagon.
Original drawing by A. Gordon Pirie based on W.G. Bagnall works drawing

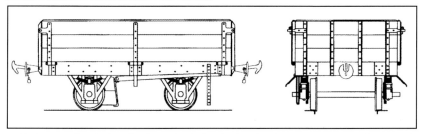

W. G. Bagnall Ltd of Stafford supplied a batch of ten brick wagons at a cost of £335 total. The drawings W554, W555 and W557 for order number 213 are dated August 1899. The wagons measured 9 ft x 5 ft with a 2 ft high body and a capacity of five tons. They were three plank drop-side open wagons with planks of 8in. The wooden planks forming the floor were made of deal. The braking mechanism consisted of a hand-lever located on only one side of the wagon connected to a wooden brake block acting on one wheel. Four grease axle boxes with brass bearings each able to carry 1½ tons were fitted. They were fitted with a "Chopper" type central combined buffer and draw-gear coupling with a chain and 2 in. diameter cast iron ball weight.

The drawings indicate that the wagons were designed with a dual gauge capability. The 3 ft gauge steel wheels were 18 in. diameter fitted on axles passing through the axle-boxes for 21 in. diameter, 4 ft 8½ in. gauge wheels also to be attached. When the wagons were delivered in December 1899, dual gauge running was still envisaged though not yet approved. The drawings are marked "1'-9" *wheel not fitted at present*". The wagons may have been delivered along with these extra parts. The proposal to make a connection with the tramways was officially declined in March 1900, so thereafter any wagons need only have been simple 3 ft gauge examples.

In October 1900 an order of five wagons was built by Messrs. Gray, Harrow and Co. Cartwrights, Coachbuilders, Blacksmiths & Wood Merchants of Charlotte Street and John Street, Aberdeen. Stated to be the first narrow gauge wagons for a light railway constructed in the north of Scotland and they were built in the space of a month and were said to be giving every satisfaction.

The photograph on the front cover shows a goods wagon which is partially visible on the same siding behind the Golf Club railcar. The design is unclear but it is different from the Bagnall example.

The wagons had the company's initials **S.B.&T. Co. Ltd.** painted on the side in high lettering. The livery is unknown. In 1906 the company possessed a total of 30 wagons.

Appendix Six

Passenger Carriages

In February 1900 the Seaton Brick & Tile Co. Ltd. purchased four old tramcars from Aberdeen Corporation Tramways. The purchase price was £15 each for three of the vehicles and £20 for the other one. They were numbers 1, 4, 5 and 6. The vehicles were former horse-drawn tramcars of Aberdeen District Tramways previously used on the Woodside route. The four-wheel double deck vehicles, each weighed approximately 2½ tons. The interior seating consisted of two wooden benches facing inwards.

Three of the tramcars were originally built in 1891 by R & J Shinnie of Union Row, Aberdeen. They had a clerestory roof which was a raised portion running longitudinally which provided extra light and ventilation to the inside compartment. It also formed a bench seat for the upper deck passengers who sat back-to-back facing outwards, and was termed "knifeboard seating".

The fourth vehicle is believed to have been a later example, constructed in 1893-1894 by R & J Shinnie. This had "garden seat" upper deck seating meaning that the benches were arranged in pairs facing forward.

After the removal of the stairways the conversion would not have required too much work since there was no structure to remove from the upper deck, just handrails and seats. New curved roofs and running boards were fitted to the vehicles. W. G. Bagnall Ltd of Stafford supplied 3 ft gauge wheel-sets for £50.

The livery of Aberdeen tramcars was dependent on which service they operated. The route colour for Woodside trams was red. This was the main body colour with window surrounds and other parts being white. It is believed that the vehicles when in service on the Strabathie Light Railway appeared in the same or similar colour scheme. From 1906 only two passenger carriages were in use.

Horse-drawn tramcar No.5 in Saint Nicholas Street. This particular vehicle was one of four purchased by the Seaton Brick & Tile Co. Ltd. for use as passenger carriages.
courtesy University of Aberdeen

Appendix Seven

Couplings

The rolling stock owned by the Seaton Brick and Tile Company Limited for use on the Strabathie Light Railway used a "Norwegian / Chopper" type coupling. This was a central combined buffer and draw-gear type of coupling consisting of a sprung buffer centrally located on the vehicle. It had a hook shaped like a meat chopper which dropped into a slot in the central buffer of the vehicle it was being coupled to. This form of coupling was not particularly strong and only really suitable for narrow gauge systems with low speeds and light loads. There was always a possibility that the hook could inadvertently jump up and uncouple, so as an additional safety measure each coupling had a chain with a two-inch diameter cast-iron ball weight which would be flipped over the hook to hold it down. The steam locomotive dispensed with the hook and chain, only having the slotted buffer part of the coupling fitted.

Chopper coupling complete with safety ball and chain

Appendix Eight

Railcars

First Railcar (Duff / Smith)

Manufactured in 1909 by John B. Duff, Coachbuilders, Cycle and Motor Manufacturers, 460, 462, 464 George Street, Aberdeen for the Murcar Links Golf Club, Limited.
It had a centre passenger compartment housing the motor with a special gearbox providing two gears for each direction. The driver powered the vehicle from here. At each end was an open coupé compartment for passengers.

Four-wheel vehicle.
Petrol powered.
20 horsepower, 4 cylinder Argyll engine.
Sliding doors and footboard on one side only.
Body varnished outside and inside.
Purchase Price £356 10s. 6d.

History and alterations.

Aug 1909	Railcar ordered from J.B. Duff
17th Dec 1909	Railcar delivered
25th Dec 1909	Railcar put into service
Jan 1910	Windows fitted in the sliding doors
Apl 1910	Warning bell fitted
Apl 1910	Couplings fitted compatible with Seaton Brick & Tile Co. rolling stock
Apl 1910	"No Smoking" notice was put up
Sep 1911	Square gear shafts substituted for original ones
Sep 1911	Lighter flywheel fitted
Nov 1911	Original three gear shafts were taken out and square ones substituted
Nov 1911	The flywheel was made lighter
Nov 1911	Duplicate driving chain purchased and left at Duff's premises as a spare.
Nov 1912	New carburettor on trial for one month
Apl 1913	Instructions issued that passenger capacity should be 36
Sep 1913	Damaged by fire

Rebuilt in 1913 by T.C. Smith & Company, Limited, Automobile & Electrical Engineers, The Aberdeen Motor Garage, 21-25 Bon Accord Street, Aberdeen.
A new body was manufactured. This had three closed compartments, with the engine housed in the middle one. The driver also operated the vehicle from here. At each end was an open coupé compartment for passengers. The original chassis, wheels and other parts were incorporated into the replacement vehicle. The original gearbox providing two gears for each direction was retained.

Four-wheel vehicle.
Petrol powered.
24-horsepower Aster engine fitted.
Petrol consumption: 10 miles per gallon.
Green livery

The vehicle was painted at various times by the manufacturer, by local painters and by the golf club. Even if the livery was green it would not always have been the same shade. Records show that it was painted in 1910, 1913, 1920 and perhaps 1937 and 1943. It is not clear which buggy is being referred to for these last two years. (The livery was red and grey according to I.D.O. Frew.) (Perhaps both vehicles were painted red in later years.)

History and alterations.

1913	Body rebuilt by T.C. Smith & Co.
1913	24-horsepower Aster engine fitted
1913	Capacity described as 43 passengers sitting plus 20 standing.
25th Dec 1913	Rebuilt car put into service
Dec 1917	Withdrawn from service under the terms of liquidation
Apl 1919	Railcar returned to scheduled service
Jun 1919	Fire extinguisher discussed
Feb 1920	Wooden barrel instead of tank discussed
Feb 1920	Instructions issued that passenger capacity should be 35
May 1920	Spare parts specially made and kept in stock
Mar 1921	Transmission gear altered by Kittybrewster Motor Works
Mar 1921	Brakes altered and strengthened by Kittybrewster Motor Works
Sep 1922	Vice and valve lifter/cutter purchased and installed in carshed
Nov 1923	Two lamps purchased
Mar 1924	Cooling tank altered, tubes installed, small chimney fitted to top of tank
Mar 1925	Engine and driving chain covered in to provide protection
Jun 1930	Fire extinguisher and bucket of sand installed under the terms of new regulations in the Petroleum Act 1929
Dec 1930	Instructions issued that passenger capacity should be 32
Jul 1932	Designated as spare car when the new Wickham railcar was delivered
May 1934	A double pinion was renewed
Apl 1941	Local boys broke 40 panes of glass so the windows were boarded up
31st Jan 1950	Withdrawn from regular service
Feb 1951	Body put to use as steward's bottle and general store
Mar 1953	Body put to use as Ladies' caddy cart store

Second Railcar (Wickham)

Manufactured by D. Wickham & Co. Ltd of Ware, Hertfordshire for Murcar Golf Club. The vehicle was of a totally enclosed design. The driver's cab was at one end in a compartment which held the engine and seating for five passengers. This had a door on the right side only. There was a main passenger compartment with seating for 35 which had one door next to the cab on the left-hand side, and one at the rear at the right-hand side. There was a duplicate set of controls at the rear end.

Maker's car number: 584
Order number: 4879
Wickham type: as drawing 906/A
24 horsepower, 4-cylinder Ford type "A" petrol engine, number 4488961

Ford clutch
Ford two-way gearbox
Wickham full reverse box
Final drive to one axle by roller chain
Four 2 ft diameter cast steel spoked wheels
Cast-iron axle boxes fitted with Skefco self-aligning bearings
Petrol consumption: 18 miles per gallon.
Livery was red (red and grey)**
22 seats *
4 roof lights in passenger compartment *
2 roof lights in rear compartment *
5 ribs on the roof *
Sheet metal sides with hardboard panelling inside *
Overall length 23 ft (approx)*
Overall height 7 ft 6 in. (approx)*
Purchase Price £600***

* Like the first railcar the second was painted by a variety of painters, and even if the livery was always red it would not always have been the same shade. Records show that it was painted in 1932, 1948 and perhaps 1937 and 1943. It is not clear which buggy is being referred to for these two years.

** These details noted and measurements taken after the car had been withdrawn from service.

*** Additional costs applied because of alterations made prior to and after delivery.

History and alterations

4th Jul 1932	Despatched from works
11th Jul 1932	Delivered and put on the tracks
Oct 1932	Inside of the roof enamelled
Oct 1932	Floor strengthened
Oct 1932	Floor lined with linoleum
Oct 1932	Hair cushions covered with REPP fitted on the seats
Apl 1933	Radiator replaced
Nov 1933	Cast-iron sprocket and chain gave way and were replaced with steel versions free of charge by Wickham & Co.
Sep 1934	One wheel collapsed so new stronger wheels were ordered for £27 10s.
Nov 1934	Wheels replaced by stronger versions
May 1935	Reconditioned 24HP Ford engine purchased so a spare would be available
Aug 1935	Valves burned out and repairs carried out
Aug 1935	A crack appeared in the rim of one of the new wheels so Wickham & Co. refunded the expenses of welding repairs which had to done locally.
Aug 1935	Leaking roof repaired by William Briggs & Sons Ltd., Asphalt Contractors & Manufacturers, Bedford Road, Aberdeen.

Mar 1936	Holes appeared in a part of the tin interior due to corrosion from the inside. After consultation with J. Joss & Sons it was decided that part of the panel should be cut and a new part welded.
Mar 1936	The brakes were renewed
Jun 1936	Troubles were experienced with the wheels. The spokes had to be welded and this was paid for by Wickham & Co. since it fell within the remit of the maintenance agreement.
Jan 1937	A new brake was fitted
Nov 1937	The two-way gear boxes were renewed owing to wear and tear
May 1939	The wheels were so flat that the flanges were cutting into the bolts of the fishplates on the track. They were re-tyred by Cassie of King Street, Aberdeen but castings were also ordered from Wickham & Co. at a cost of £14 for replacement at a later date.
Feb 1948	Two wheels machined and welded. Wickham quoted new ones at £14 11s. 9d. The repairs were found to be effective so it was decided to repair the other wheels rather than buy new ones.
Apl 1948	Wiring repaired
Apl 1948	Glass renewed
Apl 1948	The vehicle was repainted by Jim Fiddes, the driver
31st Jan 1950	Withdrawn from regular service
15-30 Jul 1950	Returned to service for a fortnight
Oct 1951	Body removed and chassis used as wagon for carrying dismantled track
Dec 1951	Chassis and engine removed by scrap company by mistake
Mar 1952	Engine returned to Murcar Golf Club to be used as a spare for tractor
Mar 1953	Body in use as a caddy cart store

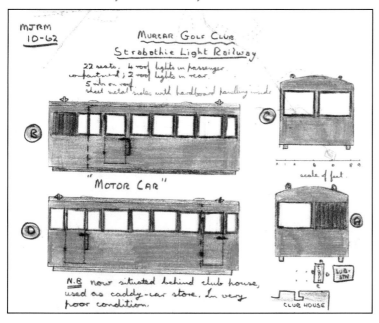

A drawing made of the Wickham railcar in 1962 when it was in use as a caddy cart store.
courtesy Mike Mitchell

Appendix Nine

Train Services and Timetables

The steam locomotive was kept overnight in the engine shed at the Bridge of Don terminus. The workmen's train would normally consist of the locomotive plus two carriages. This carried the workers from the Bridge of Don to the brickworks at Strabathie. The workmen's train returned to the terminus in the evening during the week and about midday on Saturdays. The brickworks passenger train was often used for transporting visitors to the brickworks. Also, since there was no other means of transport over the links the passenger train turned out to be extremely handy for many organisations over the years.

During the day the traffic flow was wagonloads of bricks being hauled from Strabathie brickworks to the Bridge of Don terminus and empties returning to the works. The normal load from the works was the locomotive plus five loaded wagons, each wagon with a load of four tons. After being emptied, the wagons would be available for transporting any other goods required at the brickworks. An important northbound cargo was coal which was obtained from a main line railway yard in Aberdeen. It was bagged and then carted to Bridge of Don to be transferred onto brick wagons for Strabathie.

In 1899 it was estimated that with brick traffic from Strabathie, plus coal going to the works, the volume of goods would be at least 22,000 tons per annum. After the railway was built, it was quoted that in some of the previous years, up to 1913, 25,000 tons had been carried every year, very much in line with what had been estimated.

Bulk material was also often carried in brick wagons from the Bridge of Don for Murcar Links Golf Club. This consisted of horse manure, mould for top dressing, compost, topsoil, turf, grass seed and granite chips. In the early days of construction especially this amounted to many tons, and thereafter was always required for maintenance and improvements.

The Murcar Links Golf Club course opened on Saturday 5th June, 1909. Later in the day, after the brickworks had finished business, a train service was provided by the Seaton Brick and Tile Company Limited using the locomotive and two carriages. The journey time was seven minutes.

On Saturdays only from June to December 1909 the Seaton Brick and Tile Company Limited continued to provide a service for members of Murcar Links Golf Club. At first, three trains in each direction using the locomotive hauling two carriages were advertised as a regular schedule.

June 1909 Saturdays Only
Operated by Seaton Brick & Tile Co. train for golfers.
Complete Timetable

	Depart BoD	Return
Saturdays	10.30 am	1.15 pm
"	2.00 pm	6.00 pm
"	3.00 pm	8.00 pm

Saturday 26th June, 1909
Operated by Seaton Brick & Tile Co. train for golfers.
Complete Timetable

	Depart BoD	Return
Saturdays	10.30 am	
"	1.30 pm	1.45 pm
"	2.30 pm	2.45 pm
"	4.00 pm	4.15 pm
"	7.00 pm	8.00 pm

Saturday 3rd July, 1909
Operated by Seaton Brick & Tile Co. train for golfers.
Complete Timetable

	Depart BoD	Return
Saturdays	10.30 am	
"	12.30 pm	1.45 pm
"	1.30 pm	2.45 pm
"	2.30 pm	4.30 pm
"	4.00 pm	6.15 pm
"	6.00 pm	7.45 pm

On 25th December, 1909 the J. B. Duff railcar purchased by Murcar Links Golf Club was put into regular service. The golf club timetables were frequently altered for summer and winter timetables, for daylight saving time changes, to reduce running costs and save fuel, in accordance with the wishes of members and as permitted by the Seaton Brick and Tile Company Limited. The last runs of the day were either scheduled to be at a specific time or dependent on sunset. Special last runs were also incorporated into the schedules to take caddies home at night. Extra runs were made on public holidays and for special matches as required.*

Unofficial services included picking up golfers from the Royal Aberdeen Golf Club, carrying hikers and helping out local families who lived along the route of the railway especially in winter when the roads were blocked by snow.

A timetable for the golf club railcar service was drawn up in consultation with the Seaton Brick and Tile Company Limited. The railcar could not be used at times because the brickworks train had priority. It was agreed that the railcar could be coupled onto the rear of the brickworks train. This was arranged, but until such time as the couplings on the club railcar were adapted, the brick company. agreed to carry players by their 5.20 pm train from Bridge of Don.

At the end of 1910 the Murcar Links Golf Club railcar was booked in for overhaul. A covering service was provided by the Seaton Brick and Tile Company Limited train. This became the normal procedure thereafter whenever the railcar not available. This would either be by attaching a single carriage to the goods train or using the locomotive with one or two carriages. Since the brickworks was only operating during the summer months at this particular time with fewer trains being run it could mean that the golf club could have sole use of the railway at times. At other times the club had to wait until the season was

---

* Many alterations to the rail timetables were only by a matter of five or ten minutes either way. Many of these are on record but this appendix does not attempt to show every single change.

finished in October. The brick company train would run according to the normal golf club schedule as far as possible.

A shuttle service was operated as a joint operation on Saturday, 3rd June, 1911 for an exhibition match staged between the golf professionals George Duncan and James Sherlock. The service was as follows:

Leaving Bridge of Don

12.30 pm	Seaton Brick Co. train with one carriage attached or two if necessary
12.45 pm	Golf club railcar
1.20 pm	Golf club car and Seaton Brick Co. train with two carriages attached
2.00 pm	Golf club car and Seaton Brick Co. train with two carriages attached
And every half hour afterwards	Golf club car and Seaton Brick Co. train with two carriages attached

As an indication of how frequent the service could be, on Good Friday 5th April, 1912, the railcar left every half hour for a time in the early forenoon and hourly thereafter for most of the day.

At a meeting on 18th April, 1913 the transit committee of Murcar Links Golf Club instructed the railcar driver to take not less than eight minutes for the journey, and stipulated that the car must not leave Bridge of Don terminus until the arrival of passengers by the Corporation Tramways car scheduled to meet the club car.

During the First World War a wireless station was located at Murcar. From September 1915 personnel of the Royal Navy Volunteer Reserve occupied the clubhouse. Station staff were permitted to use the golf club railcar. In December 1917 The Murcar Links Golf Club, Limited went into liquidation meaning the railcar had to be removed from service. Military personnel were then transported to the wireless station by means of the brickworks train.

In March 1918 the golf club reformed under the name of Murcar Golf Club. A timetable was organised and the train service was provided by the Seaton Brick and Tile Company Limited until April 1919. At the end of April 1919 the railcar was running again and a new timetable was formulated starting from the 26th May which now included a Sunday service.

The Seaton Brick and Tile Company Limited train had continued to provide transport for the military personnel as well as golfers but now paid Murcar Golf Club to take over the duty of transporting the wireless station personnel in the railcar. The standard arrangement at the time was for the railcar to make a double run on six nights of the week. In March 1919 a temporary arrangement came into place whereby the railcar was run for the wireless officials at 8:00 am and 1:45 pm

From 5th September, 1919 Murcar Golf Club Railcar Service

	Depart BoD	Depart Clubhouse
Weekdays	?	?
"	?	8.45 pm
Saturday	?	7.30 pm
"	?	8.45 pm

From 7th February, 1920 Murcar Golf Club Railcar Service

	Depart BoD	Depart Clubhouse
Weekdays	?	?
Saturday	9.45 am	4.15 pm
"	10.30 am	4.45 pm
"	?	5.30 pm
Sunday	?	5.30 pm

From 21st February, 1920 Murcar Golf Club Railcar Service

	Depart BoD	Depart Clubhouse
Weekdays	?	?
Saturday	9.45 am	4.15 pm
"	10.30 am	5.00 pm
"	?	6.00 pm
Sunday	?	6.00 pm

An amended timetable was put into place from 12th April, 1920. The Seaton Brick and Tile Company Limited notified the club that after 21st April, 1920 the special runs for wireless staff would no longer be required since the Admiralty were relinquishing the rooms. This did not happen as planned though. From 8th May, 1920 a new timetable was implemented. During July and August 1920, a new arrangement was entered into with the Seaton Brick and Tile Company Limited whereby they paid Murcar Golf Club for making a special run at 9.00 am and back in the morning and allowing the wireless staff to travel by the car during weekdays. This lasted until 18th August, 1920. The wireless station closed in September 1920 and in October 1920 the timetable was amended.

The following five timetables are all for 1921 and show the variations in the schedules during the course of one year.

February 1921 Murcar Golf Club Railcar Service

	Out	In
Weekdays	?	4.30 pm
"	4.45 pm	5.00 pm
Saturday	4.45 pm	5.00 pm
Sunday	1.30 pm	5.00 pm

March 1921 Murcar Golf Club Railcar Service

	Out	In
Weekdays	2.45 pm	4.15 pm
"	4.30 pm	5.00 pm
"	5.45 pm	6.00 pm
Saturday	4.30 pm	5.00 pm
"	5.45 pm	6.00 pm
Sunday	2:15 pm	6.00 pm

A national coal strike took place from April 1921 which resulted in the curtailment of some Aberdeen Corporation Tramways services in May. Murcar Golf Club hired charabancs from Campbells Ltd to run on Saturdays between Holburn Street and the Bridge of Don at a cost of 1s. per run. The railcar was to run from the Bridge of Don on Saturday at 9.45 am and 10.15 am

May 1921 Murcar Golf Club Railcar Service

	Out	In
Weekdays	2.45 pm	4.15 pm
"	4.30 pm	5.00 pm
"	5.45 pm	6.00 pm
Saturday	9.45 am	?
"	10.15 am	?
"	4.30 pm	5.00 pm
"	5.45 pm	6.00 pm
Sunday	2.15 pm	6.00 pm

October 1921 Murcar Golf Club Railcar Service
Complete Timetable

	Depart BoD	Depart Clubhouse
Weekdays	10.00 am	12.45 pm
"	1.30 pm	2.00 pm
"	2.15 pm	2.30 pm
"	2.45 pm	3.15 pm
"	3.30 pm	4.30 pm
"	4.45 pm	5.00 pm
"	5.30 pm	6.00 pm
Saturday	9.45 am	?
"	10.15 am	?
"	12.30 pm	?
Sunday	11.00 am	?
"	2.15 pm	6.00 pm

November 1921 Murcar Golf Club Railcar Service
Complete Timetable

	Depart BoD	Depart Clubhouse
Weekdays	10.00 am	12.45 pm
"	1.30 pm	2.00 pm
"	2.15 pm	2.30 pm
"	2.45 pm	3.15 pm
"	3.30 pm	4.30 pm
"	4.45 pm	5.00 pm
"	5.30 pm	6.00 pm
Saturday	9.45 am	?
"	10.15 am	?
"	12.30 pm	?
Sunday	11.00 am	?
"	1.30 pm	5.00 pm

During 1922 many small alterations were made to the golf club railcar service. The last occasion on which the Seaton Brick and Tile Company Limited train covered for the railcar which was undergoing maintenance was in December 1922. Thereafter, other alternatives had to be found by Murcar Golf Club. It was common for a charabanc to be hired from Campbell's Limited or a bus to be run by the Bydand Bus Company.

From 12th April, 1924 Murcar Golf Club Railcar Service
Saturday Timetable

	Depart BoD	Depart Clubhouse
Saturday	9.30 am	9.45 am
"	10.00 am	10.15 am
"	12.30 pm	12.45 pm
"	1.00 pm	1.15 pm
"	1.30 pm	2.00 pm
"	2.15 pm	etc
"	etc	etc

The railcar was run at times when the club steward took laundry baskets into town. In October 1926 the club professional made a request that a special run on Thursdays or Fridays at 12.45 pm to enable him to purchase supplies. It was agreed that henceforth a special journey would be made every Thursday.

In 1932 a second railcar was purchased from Messrs. D. Wickham & Company Ltd. to run the services. The older railcar was to be kept as a reserve vehicle for when the new car was out of service for maintenance. On 6th January, 1933 a new timetable was put into place.

On the outbreak of war in September 1939 petrol rationing was brought into force. A very restricted service was put in place consisting of one return trip only on Wednesdays and two trips each way on Saturday and Sunday.

September 1939 Murcar Golf Club Railcar Service
Complete Timetable

	From BoD	From Murcar
Wednesday	1.45 pm	sunset
Saturday	9.45 am	1.00 pm
"	1.45 pm	sunset
Sunday	10.00 am	1.15 pm
"	1.45 pm	sunset

The supply of petrol became more reliable and in November the timetable was improved so there was a service on every day of the week.

November 1939 Murcar Golf Club Railcar Service
Complete Timetable

	From BoD	From Murcar
Monday	1.30 pm	sunset
Tuesday	1.30 pm	sunset
Wednesday	1.30 pm	sunset
Thursday	1.30 pm	sunset
Friday	1.30 pm	sunset
Saturday	9.30 am	12.45 pm
"	1.30 pm	sunset
Sunday	9.45 am	1.00 pm
"	1.30 pm	sunset

The scheduled runs made on Monday and Friday were found to be little used though and were therefore suspended as from January 1940, but an extra journey was scheduled for Saturdays.

January 1940 Murcar Golf Club Railcar Service
Complete Timetable

	From BoD	From Murcar
Tuesday	1.30 pm	sunset
Wednesday	1.30 pm	sunset
Thursday	1.30 pm	sunset
Saturday	9.30 am	12.45 pm
"	11.30 am	?
"	1.30 pm	sunset
Sunday	9.45 am	1.00 pm
"	1.30 pm	sunset

A further 160 gallons were granted up to the period of 31st May, 1940 so an amended timetable with more journeys was approved to commence on Saturday, 13th April, 1940.

There was a requirement now to carry more passengers than normal because of petrol rationing and extra temporary club members. In March 1941 additional services were added to the timetable to accommodate these extra numbers.

March 1941 Murcar Golf Club Railcar Service
Complete Timetable

	From BoD	From Murcar
Tuesday	1.30 pm	sunset
Wednesday	1.30 pm	sunset
Thursday	1.30 pm	sunset
Saturday	9.30 am	12.45 pm
"	11.30 am	?
"	1.30 pm	?
"	2.15 pm	6.00 pm
Sunday	9.45 am	1.00 pm
"	1.30 pm	2.15 pm
"	2.30 pm	6.00 pm

The end of the war in 1945 was celebrated with the Victory Day Holiday on Saturday, 8th June, 1946. A special more frequent railcar service was arranged for that day.

Saturday, 8th June, 1946 Victory Day Holiday Service
Complete Timetable

Depart BoD	Depart Clubhouse
9.00 am	9.15 am
9.30 am	9.45 am
10.00 am	10.45 am
11.00 am	12.45 pm
1.30 pm	1.45 pm

The rail service was officially stopped on 31st January, 1950. From 1st February, 1950 a taxi service provided by W.G. Pirie running to a timetable replaced it. However, the Pirie taxi service ceased in June and the railcar service was reprieved for a fortnight. The last scheduled rail service was made by the Wickham railcar on Friday 30th June, 1950. Hilton Taxis then took over the service on 1st July, 1950 for a year.

A new contract was agreed with Clifton Taxis from 1st July, 1951. The runs were still made according to a timetable which changed according to the season and the requirements.

From December 1951 Murcar Golf Club Taxi Service

Depart BoD	Depart Clubhouse
9.30 am	?
11.00 am	12.45 pm
1.30 pm	5.00 pm

Jim Fiddes ringing the warning bell to announce the departure of the Murcar Buggy in 1948. The bell is now on display in the trophy cabinet of Murcar Links Golf Club.

courtesy Aberdeen Bon-Accord and Northern Pictorial

Appendix Ten

Golf Club Fares and Tickets

1909
3*d*. return ticket
1*d*. per run for caddies

In January 1910 member Mr John Smart offered to supply car tickets to the club after the present supply was done on condition that he was allowed to advertise on the back. He was Carrier to HM the King & HRH Prince of Wales, Deeside Carrier & Royal Mail Contractor. These were supplied in a roll of 1000 pre-numbered tickets.

In September 1911 it was brought to everybody's attention that caddies using the railcar should still be charged a penny per run. This rule had apparently fallen into disuse through some misunderstanding. A proposal was made to the effect that caddies be allowed to travel free of charge. Unfortunately, the gentleman who proposed this was absent from the next couple of meetings so the motion was dropped and the caddies had to pay their fares again.

1915
2*d*. each trip for wireless station personnel.

1918
4*d*. each way during the week
6*d*. each way on Sundays
half fare for children
Records of tickets issued to the driver in this period:

12th April, 1919:	Nos. 1001-2000 and 2001-3000.
17th June, 1919:	Nos. 3001-4000 and 4001-5000
10th July, 1919:	Nos. 5001-6000 and 6001-7000
later issues:	6001-7000, 7001-8000, 8001-9000

courtesy The W.C. Bett Ticket Collection,   *author's collection*
Birmingham Central Library

Tickets for the rail service operated by Murcar Golf Club. The ones above measure 1⁷⁄₁₆ in. x 1³⁄₃₂ in. (37 mm x 28 mm). The one on the facing page was issued in 1933.

From 1920 the tickets were printed by the Glasgow Numerical Ticket & Check Book Printing Company Limited, 31 Finnieston Street, Glasgow. Murcar Golf Club paid £2 14s. 11d. for the first delivery of 50,000 tickets in May 1920, followed by another 50,000 tickets for £2 18s. 4d. in June 1921 and a batch of 100,000 in March 1927.

October 1927
Fares decreased
2d. each way during the week
3d. each way on Sundays
½d. for caddies
No more half fares for children

The same printer in Glasgow changed its name slightly and was later known as the Glasgow Numerical Printing Company Limited. Examples of tickets from this period are either marked G.N.P. Co. Ltd. or Glasgow Numerical Ptg. Co., Ltd.

Tickets were supplied in rolls. There was no price shown and of course no destination was necessary. The largest print stated PASSENGERS CARRIED AT THEIR OWN RISK.

courtesy The Railway Magazine

November 1935
Free travel only for caddies on a list kept by the club professional

1st January, 1939
Fares increased
3d. each way during the week
4d. each way on Sundays

1st February, 1950
Taxi 6d. each run

September 1952
Taxi 9d. Single run
Taxi 1s. Double run

November 1952
Taxi 9d. each way

Appendix Eleven

Railcar Usage Figures
for the years when published

	1914			1915	
Passengers		no record	Passengers		no record
Mileage		no record	Mileage		no record
Miles per Gallon		no record	Miles per Gallon		no record
Ticket Sales		£235 15s. 3d.	Ticket Sales		no record
Deficit		£103 19s. 7d.	Deficit		£148 18s. 4d.

	1919			1920	
Passengers		no record	Passengers		26776
Mileage		no record	Mileage for Club		7360
Miles per Gallon		no record	for Wireless Stn		1692
Ticket Sales		£255 5s. 4d.	Mileage total		9052
Surplus		£133 7s. 7d.	Miles per Gallon		no record
			Ticket Sales		£479 2s. 10d.
			Surplus		£286 6s. 4d.

	1921			1922	
Passengers		31746	Passengers		29932
Mileage		8372	Mileage		10602
Miles per Gallon		11.595	Miles per Gallon		12.47
Ticket Sales		£553 10s. 8d.	Ticket Sales		£518 9s. 0d.
Surplus		£46 13s. 8d.	Surplus		£51 15s. 8d.

	1923			1924	
Passengers		30680	Passengers		24567
Mileage		12452	Mileage		12392
Miles per Gallon		14.28	Miles per Gallon		14.25
Ticket Sales		no record	Ticket Sales		no record
Surplus		no record	Surplus		no record

	1925			1926	
Passengers		26004	Passengers		25281
Mileage		12092	Mileage		11884
Miles per Gallon		no record	Miles per Gallon		no record
Ticket Sales		no record	Ticket Sales		no record
Deficit		no record	Deficit		no record

	1927			1928	
Passengers		23083	Passengers		24459
Mileage		12304	Mileage		12792
Miles per Gallon		no record	Miles per Gallon		14.33
Ticket Sales		no record	Ticket Sales		no record
Deficit		no record	Deficit		no record

1929		**1930**	
Passengers	24411	Passengers	23799
Mileage	12429	Mileage	13208
Miles per Gallon	14	Miles per Gallon	no record
Ticket Sales	no record	Ticket Sales	no record
Deficit	no record	Deficit	no record
1931		**1932**	
Passengers	24679	Passengers	no record
Mileage	14612	Mileage	no record
Miles per Gallon	no record	Miles per Gallon	13.5
Ticket Sales	no record	Ticket Sales	no record
Deficit	no record	Deficit	no record
1933		**1934**	
Passengers	24008	Passengers	19634
Mileage	15648	Mileage	17216
Miles per Gallon	16.33	Miles per Gallon	15
Ticket Sales	no record	Ticket Sales	no record
Deficit	no record	Deficit	over £300
1935		**1936**	
Passengers	16081	Passengers	14847
Mileage	no record	Mileage	no record
Miles per Gallon	17.4	Miles per Gallon	17.01
Ticket Sales	no record	Ticket Sales	no record
Deficit	£233 14s. 1d.	Deficit	£324 18s. 5d.
1937		**1938**	
Passengers	12773	Passengers	10677
Mileage	no record	Mileage	no record
Miles per Gallon	18.08	Miles per Gallon	15.6
Ticket Sales	no record	Ticket Sales	£93 11s. 0d.
Deficit	£113 12s. 5d.	Deficit	£315 14s. 7d.
1939		**1940**	
Passengers	7720	Passengers	3270
Mileage	no record	Mileage	no record
Miles per Gallon	16.18	Miles per Gallon	9.52
Ticket Sales	£108 4s. 0d.	Ticket Sales	£51 17s. 11d.
Deficit	£183 17s. 4d.	Deficit	£158 15s. 9d.
1941		**1944**	
Passengers	4610	Passengers	no record
Mileage	no record	Mileage	no record
Miles per Gallon	13.66	Miles per Gallon	no record
Ticket Sales	£61 13s. 6d.	Ticket Sales	no record
Deficit	£157 16s. 6d.	Deficit	£79 0s. 5d.

	1945			**1946**	
Passengers	no record		Passengers	no record	
Mileage	no record		Mileage	no record	
Miles per Gallon	no record		Miles per Gallon	no record	
Ticket Sales	no record		Ticket Sales	no record	
Deficit	£139 3s. 2d.		Deficit	£223 0s. 6d.	

	1947			**1948**	
Passengers	no record		Passengers	no record	
Mileage	no record		Mileage	no record	
Miles per Gallon	no record		Miles per Gallon	no record	
Ticket Sales	no record		Ticket Sales	no record	
Deficit	£217 16s. 2d.		Deficit	£258 9s. 5d.	

	1949	
Passengers	no record	
Mileage	no record	
Miles per Gallon	no record	
Ticket Sales	no record	
Deficit	£424 0s. 1d.	

Appendix Twelve

Golf Club Transit Accounts for years when published

13th January, 1910 (Estimates)

	Expenses		Income	
Mr Emslie, convenor of the transit committee submitted the following estimate of the cost of running the railcar:				
Income per annum, say £6 per week, on average of 60 passengers per day at 4d. return fare. Total			£312	- -
Interest on £360 (car and carriage) at 5 per cent	£18	- -		
Depreciation at 10 per cent	£36	- -		
Repairs	£10	- -		
Petrol@25 miles per day@10 miles per gallon @ 1s. per gallon – 2s. 6d. for 300 days	£38	15s. -		
Driver @20s. per week	£52	- -		
Lubricants	£8	- -		
Insurance	£36	5s. -		
Rent of railway	£120	- -		
Total	£319	- -		

31st October, 1919 (Actual Accounts)   Expenses   Income   Forward

	Expenses	Income	Forward
			£941 17s. 7d.
Car drawings from 14th April, 1919		£255 5s. 4d.	
Seaton Brick & Tile Co. for			
driving Wireless Officials		£130 1s. 5d.	
Stock of Petrol on hand		£4 2s. 6d.	
Total		£389 9s. 3d.	
Wages	£111 18s. 5d.		
Rent	£37 16s. 3d.		
Advertising	£2 11s. -		
Repairs	£20 - -		
Motor Spirit & Oil etc.	£61 12s. 6d.		
Hire to owner of Car	£6 10s. -		
Insurance - Third Party &			
Workmens' Compensation	£15 5s. 6d.		
Miscellaneous	- 8s. -		
Total	£256 1s. 8d.		
Difference			£133 7s. 7d.
			£1,075 5s. 2d.

31st October, 1920 (Actual Accounts)   Expenses   Income   Forward

	Expenses	Income	Forward
			£1,491 16s. -
Car drawings for year		£479 2s.10d.	
Seaton Brick & Tile Co. for			
running wireless officials		£317 8s. 7d.	
Petrol duty reclaimed		£5 1s. 6d.	
Stock of Petrol in hand			
- 153 gallons @ 3/1		£22 10s. -	
Total		£824 2s.11d.	
Less Stock in hand at			
31st October, 1919	£4 2s. 6d.		
Rent of Wayleave	£65 - -		
Wages	£219 13s. 6d.		
Petrol, Machine Oil etc	£176 7s. 3d.		
Hire of Car	£2 2s.10d.		
Repairs, cleaning materials etc	£38 19s. 8d.		
Insurance - Third Party &			
Workmens' Compensation	£21 15s.11d.		
Waterproof Cover for Car	£5 10s. -		
50,000 Car Tickets	£2 14s.11d.		
Miscellaneous	£1 10s. -		
Total	£537 16s. 7d.		
Difference			£286 6s. 4d.
			£1,778 2s. 4d.

31st October, 1921 (Actual Accounts)	Expenses	Income	Forward
			£1,651 12s. 6d.
Car drawings for year		£553 10s. 8d.	
Royal Exchange Assurance Co.			
No Claim Bonus)		£2 1s. 9d.	
Stock of Petrol in hand			
31st October, 1921		£10 16s. 8d.	
Total		£566 9s. 1d.	
Less Stock of petrol in hand			
31st October, 1920	£22 10s. -		
Rent of Wayleave	£63 15s. -		
Wages	£185 6s. 2d.		
Petrol, Machine Oil etc	£136 11s. 9d.		
Repairs and Cleaning	£64 13s.11d.		
Insurance (F.P.& W.C.A.)	£23 4s. 9d.		
50,000 Car Tickets	£2 18s. 4d.		
Advertising	£3 13s. 6d.		
Campbells Ltd for Hiring £26			
less fares received £12 13s.	£13 7s. -		
Total	£519 15s. 5d.		
Difference			£46 13s. 8d.
			£1,698 6s. 2d.

31st October, 1922 (Actual Accounts)	Expenses	Income	Forward
			£1,645 14s. 9d.
Car drawings for year		£518 9s. -	
Stock of Petrol on hand			
31st October, 1922		£5 8s. 4d.	
Total		£523 17s. 4d.	
Stock of Petrol on hand			
31st October, 1921	£10 16s. 8d.		
Rent of Wayleave	£63 15s. -		
Wages	£185 13s. 8d.		
Petrol, Machine Oil etc	£110 7s. 4d.		
Repairs and Cleaning	£36 7s. 4d.		
Insurance	£24 13s. 8d.		
Income Tax on profit made			
running wireless officials	£34 10s. -		
Advertising	- 18s. -		
Vice	£2 5s. -		
Miscellaneous	£2 15s. -		
Total	£472 1s. 8d.		
Difference			£51 15s. 8d.
			£1,697 10s. 5d.

Appendix Thirteen

Example of maintenance report on Railcar

Thur 6th Mar 1924
Murcar Car Engine
As agreed at last council meeting I had the car engine taken to pieces and removed to shop for examination and repair. The repairs completed at December 1922 were mainly new piston rings, repairs to pistons and cylinders, new valves and guides and tappets. These were found to be at this time in good workable condition except that the valves and valve seatings required abnormal adjustment. The driver was supplied with a valve lifter and cutter and instructed in their use, but little or nothing has been done, with the result that the valves are already very much worse of wear. These valves and valve seatings should be ground at least every two months and as this affects the consumption of petrol it is most important that this should be done. The valves and valve seatings have all been recut.

The cylinder cooling chambers, pipes leading to and from the cooling tank including the tank itself were quite full of corrosion, this was with difficulty removed, the parts affected having to be boiled in soda. To prevent this abnormal corrosion which was caused by extra heat in running a much increased mileage during the past year, it was decided to fill the cooling tank with tubes which will now give some considerable cooling surface and a small chimney was added to top of tank to lead the steam off. Four studs had to be bored out and replaced in cylinders owing to this corrosion. This has proved of great advantage as since the car again started running the circulation is perfect.

The bottom casing and brake hoses were not removed at December 1922 and on doing so at this time it was found that the brass gauze forming oil filters was torn, this had to be renewed and the whole casing thoroughly cleaned. The crank bearings were perhaps not in a breakdown condition but had at some previous repair been very badly fitted, the pins holding the brasses to bases were loose and some awanting, with the result that the brasses were revolving. In two cases the cranks were put together in such a way that the oil was thrown out instead of being scooped up. The pins mentioned have been fitted and shrunk in, the bearings adjusted where necessary filled with solder.

The connecting bolts have been annealed. The rubber connections and adjusting clips for metal pipes were not in good condition and on being removed would not replace, these had to be renewed.

The exhaust has been thoroughly cleaned, five seatings were planed level, two studs bored out and replaced, carburettor was also repaired.

The new magneto is working very satisfactorily, the platinum points of same which on old one used to give out every month or two are in perfect condition.

There has been no examination of the changegear for about three years and as it was desirable to have the car again running on Saturday 16th February there was no time available for this purpose. Before doing so it would be advisable if we could secure the original drawings of the gear and I have made a request of Mr Duff, George Street, who supplied the original gear. He promised to search for it but up to date this has not been found.

I might mention that since the engine was repaired on December 1922 there is not the same necessity for changing gear, and it is a fact that only in starting from south and with a full load is the low gear used so that there is now very little wear.

During the present snow storm the driver has repainted and varnished the car, he started on Saturday 1st inst. and the job took 3½ days including Sunday all day. I am sure it will be agreed that he has made a good job of it.

Signed F.W. Forbes

The giving of an honorarium of £2 to Mr Forbes' engineer and £1 to the driver for late work in repairing the engine of the car was approved of.

Appendix Fourteen

Murcar Buggy Drivers

December 1909 – January 1910	John B. Duff and Allan Grant
January 1910 – August 1911	Allan Grant
August 1911 – November 1912	McRobb
November 1912 – February 1913	Smith
February 1913 – December 1917	Name(s) Unknown
December 1917 – April 1919	Railcar out of service after liquidation of the club.
April 1919 – June 1925	Thomas Sim
September 1920	Trotter (of the Bridge of Don Garage) acting as relief driver for one week in 1920.
June 1925 – November 1929	John Sutherland
June 1926	Thomas Sim (for one week when John Sutherland got married)
April 1927 - ?	James Gibb (acting as relief driver for one half day each week and one Sunday each month)
November 1929 – July 1941	James Fiddes
April 1931 - ?	David Gibb (acting as relief driver for one half day each week and one Sunday each month)
May 1932 – September 1939	William C. Smith (acting as relief driver one half day each week and one Sunday each month)
July 1941 – July 1942	George Jolly
July 1941 – July 1942	James Fiddes (acting as relief driver, one Sunday each month)
July 1942 – August 1942	James Fraser
August 1942 – June 1950	James Fiddes